DISCOVER
SCOTLAND

DISCOVER
SCOTLAND

Bryn Frank

JOHNSTON & BACON
LONDON & EDINBURGH

THE FAMOUS GROUSE
COUNTRY OF ORIGIN - SCOTLAND. NOTED FOR
ITS CHARACTER AND DISTINGUISHED APPEARANCE

Quality in an age of change.

Contents

Text by Bryn Frank

A Johnston & Bacon book published by
Cassell Ltd.
35 Red Lion Square, London WC1R 4SG
and Tanfield House, Tanfield Lane, Edinburgh EH3 5LL
and at Sydney, Auckland. Toronto, Johannesburg
an affiliate of
Macmillan Publishing Co.
New York

© Johnston & Bacon, a division of Cassell Ltd., 1979

First Published 1979

ISBN 0 7179 4247 3

Printed in Great Britain by Morrison & Gibb Ltd.,
London and Edinburgh

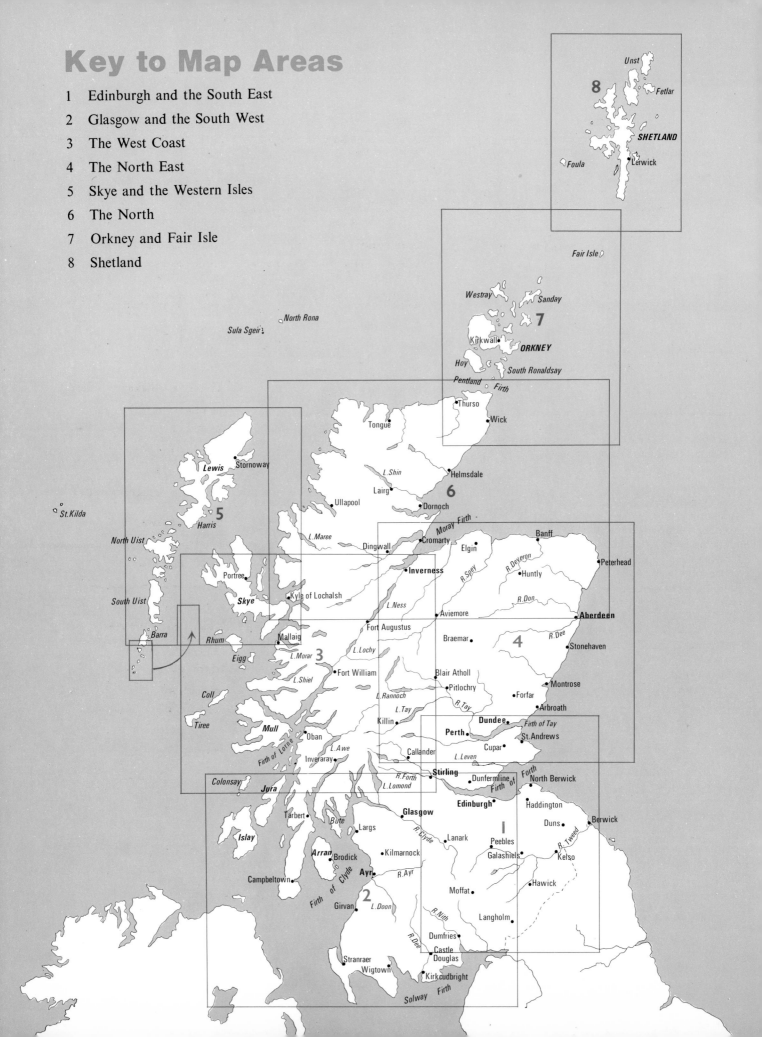

Key to Map Areas

1 Edinburgh and the South East

2 Glasgow and the South West

3 The West Coast

4 The North East

5 Skye and the Western Isles

6 The North

7 Orkney and Fair Isle

8 Shetland

Map Legend

LEGEND	LÉGENDE	ZEICHENERKLÄRUNG
Motorway with junction number and service area	Autoroute avec numéro d'échangeur et station service	Autobahn mit Nummer der Anschlußstelle und Servicestelle
Motorway junction with limited interchange	Echangeur d'autoroute à échange limité	Anschlußstelle mit begrenztem Richtungswechsel
Distances between junctions	Distances entre les échangeurs	Entfernungen zwischen Anschlußstellen
Motorway under construction	Autoroute en construction	Autobahn im Bau
Motorway projected	Autoroute projetée	Geplante Autobahn
Primary routes single and dual carriageway	Itinéraires principaux à une seule chaussée et à chaussées séparées	Häuptverbindungsstraßen normal und mehrbahnig
Other A class roads single and dual carriageway	Autres routes principales à une seule chaussée et à chaussées séparées	Sonstige Hauptstraßen Klasse A normal und mehrbahnig
B class roads	Routes secondaires	Straßen Klasse B
Major bypasses under construction	Routes de contournement en construction	Hauptumgehungsstraßen im Bau
Unclassified roads	Routes non classifiées	Nebenstraßen
Distances in miles	Distances en milles	Entfernungen in Meilen
Steep gradients	Pentes fortes	Steile Steigungen
Car Ferries	Bac à voitures	Autofähren
Principal airports	Aéroports principaux	Hauptflughäfen
Principal heights in feet	Hauteurs principales en pieds	Berghöhen in Füße
National Parks and National Forest Parks	Parcs nationaux et parcs forestiers nationaux	Nationalparks und Nationalwaldparks
AA and RAC telephone boxes	Cabines téléphoniques pour l'AA et le RAC	AA oder RAC Telefon
Race courses	Champs de course	Rennplätze
Motor racing circuits	Circuits de course	Motorrennbahnen
Regional and county boundaries	Limites de régions et de comtés	Regional-und Grafschaftsgrenzen
Canals	Canaux	Kanäle
Railways with stations	Voies ferrées avec gares	Eisenbahnen mit Bahnhöfen
Sandy beaches	Plages de sable	Sandstrände
Sailing areas	Zones de navigation à voile	Segelgebiete
Major golf courses	Terrains de golf	Hauptgolfplätze
Youth hostels	Auberges de jeunesse	Jugendherbergen
Places of Interest	Curiosités	Sehenswürdigkeiten
Information centres	Centres d' information	Informationszentren

Junctions   M8   Service Areas
HARTHILL

A9 Dual Carriageways

A861 Dual Carriageways

B920

Distances in miles 8

EDINBURGH

BEN NEVIS 4406 ▲

Glen More

INGLISTON

Scone Palace

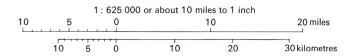

1 : 625 000 or about 10 miles to 1 inch

10   5   0   10   20 miles

10 5 0   10   20   30 kilometres

5

Introduction

It is difficult to be indifferent to Scotland; it is a country which engenders passions. Many an Englishman has returned from a rained-off Highland holiday to the soft and Sybaritic south and vowed never to cross the border again – while his neighbour, who was still there when the rain stopped, saw some of the most dramatic landscapes in Europe suddenly illuminated, and returns for his holidays year after year.

The weather, though, is not so much a curse as a characteristic of the country. Nobody will deny the impact of those glorious moments when a rain storm moves away and the sun transforms the country from the monochrome of mist and drizzle to glorious technicolour: but to see the island of Jura in heavy mist from a vantage point on Islay, when Force 10 winds are whipping up the Sound that separates them, or the great mass of Stirling Castle, once the most important in Scotland, looking on a misty November afternoon much as it did hundreds of years ago, is to have a sudden insight into the tragic and turbulent past of this, for the southerner, vast and underpopulated country.

The Scots love to hear their homeland praised by outsiders. For in spite of the resurgence of nationalistic pride in the last few years, and despite commercially-based and musical allusions to Scotland's 'bonniness', they are very modest about it. There are, of course, good practical reasons for that: very few citizens of Glasgow or Edinburgh can make a living from Scotland's hills and moors or from the Burns or Scott legends. A local phenomenon, incidentally, is the enthusiasm that is expressed for things Scottish by those Englishmen who have made their home over the border.

The question of whether tourism is good for a country is a hotly debated one, though in Scotland the 'antis' have a hard time of it. There is no real danger of overcrowding – though visitors to certain events or localities may well disagree. And many tourist developments have benefited from the resident population.

I suspect that if you stopped ten incoming tourists at Heathrow Airport who were on their first ever visit to Britain, and asked them where Scotland was in relation to the rest of the United Kingdom, they would say, in their respective languages, that it was 'the little bit of mainland at the top of the map', little realising, I am sure, that Scotland is two-thirds the size of England. But the population is tiny in comparison – just five million – so it will come as no surprise to hear that the old county of Sutherland, which still retains its identity in spite of having been swallowed by the administrative region called 'Highland', has so few people to the square mile that it compares with the 'Frontier' designation used for certain remote areas of the USA while it was being colonised.

Paisley Abbey

If you intend using this book as a practical guide, some general comments will be helpful. Do not try to cover too much ground in too short a time. Do book your car on the inter-island ferries if you are using a popular route at a busy time. Similarly, do book your accommodation in advance. Read the map and the ferry timetables, so that you are not attempting the impossible in a limited time. Do buy guide-books as you go. Some of them are very well produced, and that fairy-tale tower house on Royal Deeside or that Argyll fishing village will be much more memorable for an authoritative brochure.

You will be able to enjoy much better meals in restaurants and hotels than a few years ago. (You may think that mutton pie, thick chips and tinned peas are the nectar of the gods, but at least you will nowadays have some alternatives in even a run-of-the-mill restaurant.) Do bear in mind though, that it is unreasonable to expect large selections of fresh vegetables or fresh fruit in some areas: one of the commonest and most excusable complaints to be heard on the Inner and Outer Hebrides, in particular, is the high cost of importing the kind of goods that most holidaymakers take for granted. So order local rather than imported produce when having a meal in a hotel or restaurant – though it is fair to warn that 'local trout' may actually come from a fish-farm.

Read up a little of Scots history, so that at least you know why so many people call their children Bruce!

Do give public transport a chance, for it is surprising how far you can get on the train or the bus, and how limited you are in the west if you don't use the car and passenger ferries. The Scottish ferry network may be only one-tenth of the size of Norway's, whose west coast is in some ways comparable, but it is efficient, and for most visitors offers a treat in itself. Bad sailors will probably opt for planes to the isles of Harris and Lewis, and to Orkney and Shetland, but only the chronically sea-sick will be upset by the trip from the mainland of Oban to Mull (for *real* cowards there's even a 10-minute alternative from Lochaline, across the Sound of Mull), and the 45-minute crossing from Ardrossan to Brodick, on Arran, is bearable even in bad weather.

Even if you are a natural optimist, do expect the whole gamut of weather conditions on your trip. As one distinguished hotelier in the far north-west says in his brochure, it can change 'from Aegean to Arctic in the space of a week'. So take waterproof clothing of good quality and, especially, plenty of changes of socks and footwear. And remember that walking can be a most rewarding activity in the Scottish countryside.

If this guide succeeds in, not encompassing, but at least conveying the vastness of Scotland, we will have achieved something. To many visitors, the image of Scotland is a clichéd one. Tartan and tweed and the sound of a piper can play an important part in the ambience, of course. But it would be a shame if the many thousands of tourists came away laden with tweeds and Edinburgh rock but without a real sense of the immense variety of Scottish scenery, the individual and often jealously guarded character of the different regions and islands, and at least a sketchy knowledge of some of the main events in Scottish history, to make more sense of many geographical features and man-made landmarks. For it is easier and quicker than most people realise to see the remoter corners of the country: holiday cottages seem to get cheaper the further north or west you go, roads are often astonishingly well-surfaced and long distance train travel can be more inspiring than anywhere else in Britain.

Robert Burns' cottage

If *Discover Scotland* makes you want to get off the well-trodden tourist track, producing it will have been worthwhile. Because it surveys all of Scotland, it has given us the chance to include places that are personal favourites and not just the standard tourist guide entries. It allows us, too, to look at outlying parts of the country, including the islands, and to include some detailed practical information, with facts and figures about booking hotels, staying in youth hostels, where to buy Scottish crafts, hill walking, mountaineering, where and how to eat well and inexpensively. It includes also a 'budget holiday' guide for young people – as well as those fellow-creatures who have, perhaps, lived not wisely but too well for several days in a four-star Scottish castle, and need to drop their sights for a while and go to 'a B-and-B'. (Note, however, that if you are lucky enough to

Crinan Canal

find a 'treasure' among landladies you will probably never go back to a hotel!) There is plenty of moderately-priced accommodation, and Scotland has a higher proportion of beautifully situated hotels than anywhere else in Britain. If you cannot find a room with a view of a lochan or a glen, a fishing harbour or a golf course, you may not be reading your map or your hotel guide properly.

With Sumburgh Airport on Shetland 1000 miles from London, further away than Milan, and Inverness ten hours away by train, getting to Scotland and what it costs is of prime importance. So we have devoted a section to that, with a mini-dossier about plane, train, bus and coach travel to Scotland, as well as how to get around once you cross the border, plus information on car hire, ferries and canal boats, holiday cruises – including those to remote, rarely visited islands on which, it seems, human beings are allowed only on sufferance by guillemots, fulmars and seals.

On a sunny Sunday in July or August, the A82 through Glencoe is not unlike the North Circular in London during an average rush-hour. Likewise the A9 through Aviemore and Carrbridge in a good February or March – 'good', that is, for skiers. Those attractively, not tortuously, twisting roads through the Highlands look tempting on the map and when traffic is light are a pleasure to drive on. But the company of dozens of assorted lorries, holiday trailers and delivery vans is uncongenial. Go there in April, May, September, or October, however – outside school holidays and Bank Holidays – and you can be your very own monarch-of-the-glens.

Off the main north/south routes, of course, life on the open road is much easier: I have been on Skye on a sunny Sunday in late summer and have been so alone on the important road between Armadale and Broadford that I began to wonder whether war had been declared and the indigenous and visiting population had gone to ground.

This book aims to make travelling and touring in Scotland easier, to become a valuable road reference and gazetteer; and we have tried also to put over the flavour of the best of Scotland. You will at least discover the difference between blended whisky and malt, why the Loch Ness monster is not the only creature believed to lurk among the lochs of the Highlands, why Edinburgh is commonly known as 'Auld Reekie', and why taking the 'high road' or the 'low road' has nothing to do with the new by-pass.

Edinburgh and the South East

Few visitors will find themselves in this part of Scotland without visiting Edinburgh, and few capital cities in Europe can have such a pleasant approach, particularly from the south. Edinburgh is one of the great European capitals. It is not a museum piece, although it is architecturally and culturally on a par with any other city in Britain – and not just on account of its internationally famous annual Festival. It has been the capital of Scotland since 1437, and it has a decidedly regal and self-assured air about it – to the intense annoyance, it must be admitted, of many Scots living in less prosperous and more remote parts of the country.

Whether or not you visit Edinburgh at Festival time – and the city has a seemingly endless capacity for absorbing more and more visitors every year – you need to set aside two or three days to see even the principal tourist attractions. Edinburgh Castle, whose silhouette at sunset has provided the front cover for many a Scottish calendar is a must; and not to be missed are the 'Royal Mile' – the historic route that links the Castle with the Palace of Holyroodhouse, the Museum of Childhood, the Wax Museum, Princes Street, Charlotte Square and the New Town, the art galleries, St Giles' Cathedral, where John Knox once preached fire and brimstone, the Scott Monument and much else.

There are many people in London who would be surprised to hear that hundreds of foreign visitors, mainly from North America, fly direct to Scotland to see Edinburgh and some of the surrounding country without even going south to England at all. As a capital city, Edinburgh makes a very good symbol for Scotland, particularly a Scotland that has found a new self-confidence in recent years. North Sea oil was simply the catalyst it needed.

H.V. Morton, probably the best-ever writer on Scotland, and one of the very few travel writers who have achieved the status of best-sellers, has a genius for summing up the essence of a place, and this is how he captures the atmosphere of Arthur's Seat, high above the historic city: 'But always will I remember . . . Edinburgh in the evening. The sun goes down and dusk falls. I feel conscious that I should descend to fashionable Georgian levels, but that, to me, is an unreal Edinburgh. I like to linger in the dark, where winds whistle like swords and darkness creeps with an air of conspiracy.'

Even visitors whose main destination is Edinburgh, at Festival time or any other, should take a couple of days off to explore the surrounding countryside. The south east of Scotland, by which we mean Edinburgh, Fife, the Lothians, and the Borders, or, to use the pre-1975 county names, Fife, West, Mid and East Lothian, Berwickshire, Peeblesshire, Selkirkshire and Roxburghshire, are closer to the heart of Scotland's turbulent history than the lonely moors and the prosperous green and wooded farms of the interior of the region might suggest. Here are the great Border Abbeys of Melrose, Jedburgh, Dryburgh and Kelso, brooding castles like Tantallon, Crichton, Hermitage, and some of the finest historic houses in the whole of Scotland: Traquair House, Falkland Palace, Hopetoun House. Here too is a concentration of small old towns: the picture-postcard fishing port of Crail, beautifully preserved Culross, St Andrews (as pleasant as Oxford or Cambridge without the awful traffic) Haddington, Gullane, Pittenweem, Jedburgh itself, Lauder, and, right on the Northumberland border, on the River Tweed, the town of Coldstream, a happy marriage of stone houses and tall trees.

For the sake of neatness we have included Perth and Stirling in this section. This is something that Perth might resent, but it has probably grown used to having its autonomy usurped: it is said to have been the capital of Scotland for hundreds of years, with many kings crowned at nearby Scone, only to have lost even its status as a county seat in the local government reorganisation of 1975. The most immediate but probably the most lasting impression of Perth for the majority of visitors is of the wide, tree-lined River Tay, with elegant houses on each bank: a busy but civilised place, with room to breathe, and reminiscent, too, of parts of Georgian Edinburgh.

Stirling boasts one of the three or four most famous castles in Britain. It was the main residence of several of the Stuart kings, and Mary Queen of Scots was brought here to be crowned when she was a small child. There are dramatic views over the surrounding countryside from the castle walls. Stirling is an important commercial centre, and is a good base for touring the Trossachs – a microcosm of much that is best in Scottish scenery for the visitor who has limited time for sightseeing.

Edinburgh Castle

Since the Border country will, for most people, merely be a preliminary to apparently more exciting things to the north, few people will make their touring base at Kelso, Jedburgh, Hawick, Lauder or Peebles. But a holiday in the Borders would be well worthwhile, for this is an area of great historic interest and, apart from the main north/south trunk roads, it is quiet and attractive. For the purposes of this guide, it will be easiest to deal with the Borders via the various routes towards Edinburgh — each of which is worth lingering on and exploring.

The main approach roads to Scotland are the A74 north of Carlisle, the A1, which runs close to the east coast, the A697, the A68 and the A7. Several interesting places lie on the A697 and the A68, especially, and drivers who opt for approaching Edinburgh by one of these can, by making detours, see a great deal. (Driving to Scotland via the A68, or returning south by that road has, incidentally, the added advantage of showing one some of the most attractive parts of Northumberland.)

1   The A697 — Coldstream, Kelso and Duns

The countryside between the *Cheviot Hills* and the *Lammermuir Hills* bristles with castles; among them *Duns Castle* at Duns (not open to the public), and *Roxburgh Castle* near Kelso.

Duns, a small market town that was formerly the county town of Berwickshire, is said to be the birthplace of John Duns Scotus, the 13th-century philosopher. The town was completely destroyed by English invaders in 1545. It was rebuilt in about 1590. Duns lies on the A6112 from Coldstream. Between Duns and Berwick along the A6105, Chirnside is a beautifully situated straggling village. And on the border, but in Scotland, Ladykirk, on the B6470, has a church that was built by James IV in 1500 in gratitude for having survived a near-drowning here.

Between Duns and Earlston lies Greenlaw, with pleasant views of the Lammermuir Hills. *Hume Castle*, ten miles north of Kelso on the B6364, was the original seat of the Home family, the best known of whom in this century is Lord Home, the former Conservative Prime Minister. The castle is open by appointment only. The Home family seat is now *The Hirsel*, south along the A697 at Coldstream.

Coldstream, the first town in Scotland that many visitors see, lies on the north bank of the River Tweed, which at this point forms the border with England. The *Coldstream Guards* were originally raised here. The Hirsel, whose grounds are open to the public, is two miles to the north.

West of Coldstream runs the A698, linking three important Border towns — Kelso, Jedburgh and Hawick. Jedburgh and Hawick are better known to visitors because they both lie on north/south routes, respectively the A68 and the A7.

Kelso has been described as 'the most beautiful town in Scotland'. There are some exceptionally attractive old houses, and the bridge over the Tweed was the model for the Waterloo Bridge built in London in 1811. The ruins of *Kelso Abbey* are in the centre of the town, and to the north is *Floors Castle*, open to the public from May to September, excepting Fridays and Saturdays. Kelso racecourse is on the outskirts of the town.

On the Northumbrian border, south east of Kelso, on the B6352, are Kirk Yetholm and Town Yetholm, described in some guidebooks as 'the double village'. The *Pennine Way*, the longest officially designated footpath in northern Britain ends here amid rolling green country that is neither hill nor mountain, but whose feeling of remoteness belies its nearness to the bustling small towns of Kelso and Coldstream.

2   The A68 — Jedburgh, Melrose, Lauder

The A68 crosses the English border at *Carter Bar*. The road divides here, and one can, if preferred, approach Hawick north-westwards via the A6088, through a stretch of the *Border Forest Park*. About a mile south of Bonchester Bridge are the remains of an Iron Age hill fort, and ruins of houses built in Roman times.

From Carter Bar there are excellent views of vast stretches of lowland Scotland. There could be no better way to see Scotland for the first time — assuming that the weather is clear and the visibility good.

Jedburgh is an ancient, compact town full of historical interest. You could be forgiven for getting no further than this on your first trip towards Edinburgh. The red sandstone Abbey above the *Jed Water* is mainly 14th- and 15th-century, with even earlier remains. This was as vulnerable as all the rich Border Abbeys, and is now a picturesque ruin. Mary Queen of Scots stayed in Jedburgh on a visit to the Assizes in 1566 at what came to be known as *Mary Queen of Scots House*. The house is open to the public. The castle was built at about the same time as the Abbey, and the prison which replaced it is now a museum. *Canongate Bridge* dates from the mid-12th century: it is one of the oldest bridges in Scotland.

Just north of Ancrum, which is about two miles north of Jedburgh on the A68, the *Battle of Ancrum Moor* between the English and the Scots was fought in 1545: the English raiders were repulsed.

Dryburgh Abbey, just north of St Boswells, is one of the best preserved abbeys in Scotland, marvellously situated on a bend in the River Tweed. Even a casual visitor gets a vivid impression of day to day life in a great monastery during the 12th and 13th centuries.

Melrose is worth the detour of approximately two miles along the A6091, with the *Eildon Hills* immediately to the west, giving just a hint of the wild, high country that lies further west beyond Selkirk and Innerleithen.

If *Jedburgh Abbey* adds extra interest to a historic town, and *Dryburgh Abbey* is sufficiently well preserved to see how life was lived in a monastery, *Melrose Abbey* is the most beautiful of all the Border Abbeys. It has been heavily restored during this century, but not at the expense of the superb original decorative stonework and sculptures. Next to the Abbey are the *Priorwood Gardens*, open to the public. From the town there are pleasant walks into the Eildon Hills.

Melrose is an attractive old town, with several 16th- and 17th-century houses incorporating carved stones taken from the Abbey before people's attitudes to ancient monuments became more enlightened.

Rugby Union is played extensively in the Border country, and it was in Melrose that the very first game of the super-fast seven-a-side rugby originated.

North on the A68, Earlston was the home of the 13th-century poet and seer, *Thomas the Rhymer*, who correctly foretold several major episodes in Scottish history. Beyond the village, the A68 to Lauder along Lauderdale is fast and fairly straight, and a short stop at Lauder itself is worthwhile. If you wish to break your journey overnight there are three or four comfortable hotels near the main road. The town has several unusual old buildings: the town hall was once a tolbooth and a prison, and a couple of the inns reveal to the sharp-eyed observer traces of their past as important coaching inns on this, one of the main roads to Edinburgh for the last several hundred years. On the outskirts of Lauder, on *Leader Water*, is *Thirlestane Castle*, originally built in about 1590 and incorporating a 14th-century fortress. The present red sandstone structure was altered in the late 17th century for the Duke of Lauderdale. The castle is not open to the public.

Beyond Lauder the A68 begins to climb to nearly 1200 feet and at *Soutra Hill*, among the *Lammermuir Hills*, drivers on this road enjoy yet another magnificent view, this time of Edinburgh itself and the *Firth of Forth*.

Just off the A68, four miles north of Dalkeith, *Craigmillar Castle* dates from the 14th century and was a favourite retreat of Mary Queen of Scots. It has been altered considerably but is still an excellent example of a castle of its period. The castle is open to the public.

Shortly beyond here the road becomes part of the network of commuter routes that fan out from Edinburgh.

3   The A7 — Langholm, Hawick, Selkirk, Galashiels

The A7 north of Carlisle rises quickly into the dark hills that most first-time visitors to Scotland expect to see. But the first Border town is Canonbie, just two miles into Scotland, and this lies among fertile green farming country, on the banks of the *River Esk*. Just north of Canonbie is the ruin of one of the 'castles' of a famous Border country outlaw, Johnny Armstrong of Gilnockie, who was hanged at Teviothead with his gang of robbers on the orders of James V.

Langholm, on the Esk, is six miles from the Border. It is an important market town for sheep farmers. The historic *Common Riding* is held here every July. This is a fair whose origins were to mark the boundary of the town by riding along them to inspect possible damage.

Hermitage Castle is accessible via an unclassified road to the west of Burnfoot, or, more directly, north of Newcastleton on the B6399. The exterior of this castle, being conveniently well preserved, figured in the film *Mary Queen of Scots*. Mary visited this remote castle to see Bothwell during 1566. It is open to the public.

Thomas Telford, the great engineer and bridge and road builder, was the son of a Border shepherd and was born in a cottage on *Meggat Water*, which can be seen in lonely moorland country north of the B709.

Hawick has the oldest livestock auction in Britain, and another of its claims to fame is its men's prowess at Rugby Union. It is a game not associated in many southerners' minds with Scotland, but the Borders region has always produced many of the stars of the game at the highest level. From Hawick, the A6088 ascends gradually to the border, just touching the edge of the Borders Forest Park.

Near Ashkirk, between Hawick and Selkirk, is the landmark of *St Ninian's Well*, a place where early Christians were baptised. The Well is near the parish church on an unclassified road towards Roberton, south west of the village.

Selkirk suffered in the Border wars that reached their height in the early 16th century. The site of the *Battle of Flodden Field* is just over the English border. Over 80 men from Selkirk alone were at the battle but only one returned. Mungo Park, the explorer, was born near here, and there is a statue to him in the High Street. There is also a statue to Sir Walter Scott, the novelist. This part of Scotland is often nicknamed 'Scott Country' because of his associations with it. Scott's great mansion, *Abbotsford House*, was created from a farmhouse he bought in 1811, but gutted and rebuilt in 1820. The house, which lies just off the A7, south of the junction with the A72, is much visited. Scott has no more fervent admirer than H. V. Morton, who says in *In the Search for Scotland*: 'Scott was, and is forever, the King of the Border. No man can see the Eildon Hills or look at the long sweep of the Lammermuirs without remembering him; no man can hear the gurgling of a Border burn or watch the river mist lift in the morning from Teviot or Tweed with no thought for the man who knew this country better than any before or after him'.

Galashiels is an industrial town famous for its annual *Braw Lads Gathering*, which, though a 20th century institution, is a nonetheless lively pageant and carnival held in early summer.

The study of Abbotsford, the Borders home of Sir Walter Scott. The novels may be less fashionable than formerly, but the Scott legend lives on.

Some visitors will want to travel to Edinburgh via Peebles (see below). The more direct route, along the A7, passes through the village of Stow. Eight miles north of Galashiels, and a pleasant place to break your journey, there is an unusually attractive 19th-century church, and opposite this, a rare packhorse bridge. The village is attractively situated on *Gala Water*.

The most important landmark on this road, though entry is not permitted to the public, is *Borthwick Castle*, from which Mary Queen of Scots had to take flight disguised as a page-boy after her wedding to Lord Bothwell.

Entry is actively encouraged, however, to *Dalhousie Castle* (pronounced Dalhoosie), about a mile west of the A7 via the B704. This castle is now a luxurious hotel. At *Dalhousie Courte*, very popular 'medieval banquets' are held.

4 West of Hawick to Innerleithen and Peebles: Moffat

The B711 west of Hawick is worth exploring if time allows. It is a most attractive route towards one of Scotland's most celebrated and historic houses, *Traquair House*. The road runs through lonely moorland country as far as the A708; from the A708 take the B709, through higher-lying moorland towards Traquair, which is barely six miles from the town of Peebles.

The main gates at Traquair House (just south of Innerleithen, a straggling village on the Tweed) will remain closed until, it is said, a descendant of Bonnie Prince Charlie, a Stuart, ascends to the throne. The present owner of the house, Peter Maxwell Stewart, brews his own beer and sells it on the premises. Traquair is said to be the oldest continuously inhabited house in Scotland. Over the centuries, no fewer than 29 English and Scottish monarchs have visited the building.

Peebles is a good touring centre. Formerly the county town of Peeblesshire, it is well known among early summer visitors for its *Beltane Festival*, or 'Riding the Marches' (see Langholm, above). It is a spaciously laid out, stone-built town on the River Tweed. The fishing on the Tweed, incidentally, is excellent.

Less than a mile west of Peebles, on the banks of the Tweed, is *Neidpath Castle*, besieged by Cromwell during the Civil Wars, for it was an important northerly Royalist stronghold. The castle, part of whose walls are twelve feet thick, is the property of the Earl of Wemyss and March. It is open to the public.

The A703 from Peebles to Penicuik (pronounced Pennycook) joins the A701 ten miles north of Peebles, and is therefore a direct and fairly fast route into the heart of Edinburgh. The A701 runs south towards Moffat. This used to be one of Scotland's few spa towns in the 18th and early 19th centuries. Its wide main street and a hint of old-fashioned elegance and spaciousness about a few of its shops make Moffat an attractive place that is a good touring base for at least two or three days. The drive across high moorland country via the A701 or the A703 is most impressive.

5 The A1 — along the coast to Dunbar and through East Lothian

The A1 north of Berwick-upon-Tweed runs close to the main London–Edinburgh railway line, and drivers will often see Inter-City trains speeding north or south as they motor through the pleasant countryside that lies between the sea and the *Lammermuir Hills*. These, along with the *Pentland Hills* and the *Moorfoot Hills*, provide a breathing space for the citizens of Edinburgh and create a perfect approach to the metropolis.

On the coast, St Abbs is a charming little village, and there are glorious cliffs at *St Abbs Head*, and large colonies of seabirds.

Dunbar is a popular, rather fashionable holiday resort. There are some very distinguished old buildings — including the *Town House*, the longest-serving public building in Scotland. In more troubled times Mary Queen of Scots stayed in the castle with Darnley after the murder of Rizzio, and then with Bothwell after the murder of Darnley.

Haddington owes a lot to the foresight of people with sympathy for old buildings. It is an outstandingly well-preserved town which was, until the mid-1970s, the administrative centre of East Lothian. It is well worth at least a complete day's investigation. There are 129 buildings listed as 'of historic or architectural interest'. The street plan is medieval, and there are buildings of all periods, though the best of them are probably those which date back to the 18th century. But they are not museums: this is a superb example of a well-preserved past that adds colour and interest to contemporary urban life.

Between Dunbar and Haddington is East Linton, near the A1 but by-passed, a pleasant village worth a stop. Near here is *Preston Mill*, now in the care of the National Trust for Scotland. It is open daily, and well worth a visit. Near the mill is the famous *Phantassie Doocot* (dovecote), 400 years old and built of stone.

Beyond Haddington, the A1 continues to Edinburgh, passing close to Prestonpans, which gets its name from the sea-salt pans that existed here for 700 years. The *Battle of Prestonpans*, 21 September 1745, when Bonnie Prince Charlie and his Highlanders routed the troops under Sir John Cope, was fought nearby. An alternative route from Haddington to the capital is to take the A6093 through Pencaitland — on Tyne Water — and then the A68 between Pathhead and Dalkeith.

On the coast, the holiday and golfing resorts of Gullane and North Berwick are agreeably 'out on a limb'. There is an abrupt contrast with the gentle, rolling farmland country and the brooding *Tantallon Castle*, right on the coast above sheer cliffs nearly 100 feet high. The castle, open to the public, was a stronghold of the powerful Douglas family, and it withstood many sieges until it was partly demolished in the Civil War of the 1650s.

Though North Berwick and several villages nearby are within the Edinburgh commuter belt, they are also popular seaside resorts. North Berwick is an 'ancient burgh' that was developed in the 19th century without detracting from its

Preston Mill, in the care of the National Trust for Scotland, is the last working water mill in the country to use the original equipment. It lies near the picturesque village of East Linton.

charm. The *Marine Hotel* is a reminder of the glories of the railway age. Happily, there are still trains to the town from Edinburgh. The *Marine* is a three-star hotel, but there are several other reliable hotels, and much in the way of guest house accommodation, bed and breakfast facilities, self catering, caravan and camping sites.

Two miles west of North Berwick is the coastal park of *Yellowcraig*, where there is a superb beach, a nature trail, and many uncommon species of birds. Even the caravan site here won a *Civic Trust Award*.

Another worthwhile excursion from North Berwick is out to the *Bass Rock*. Landing is only permitted to *bona fide* naturalists, but there are summer pleasure trips from North Berwick to see and hear (for the sound of the seabird colonies is almost deafening) this great landmark that rises over 350 feet out of the sea. Permission to land on the island must be obtained from Mr F. Marr, who operates the boat trips from North Berwick.

About two miles west of North Berwick is Dirleton, in the shadow of a great ruined 13th-century castle. This castle, too, succumbed to the power of Cromwell's troops during the Civil War. Dirleton is one of the contenders for the title of 'most beautiful village in Scotland'.

West of Dirleton is Gullane, which has good sandy beaches and several golf courses.

Edinburgh

When George IV visited Edinburgh in 1822 he caused a great deal of gossip by wearing pink tights with a short kilt. But this is a sophisticated city, and such things were and are taken in its stride.

It is not always easy to time one's arrival in Edinburgh, but it is a lucky traveller who checks into his hotel in the capital shortly before dusk, summer or winter, and walks down *Princes Street* from the east end, with the *Castle* and the tall terraced houses of the *Royal Mile* silhouetted against the sky at the far side of *Princes Street Gardens* and the lights of the most elegant shops in the city to his right. It is the best time of day, too, to walk among the gracious houses of *Charlotte Square*, part of the 18th-century *New Town* that was initially planned by a brilliant 23 year old architect, *James Craig*, in 1767. Through half-closed eyes it is easy to imagine life in this spacious corner of the city as it was lived 200 years ago. By daylight one can visit *The Georgian House*, at 7 Charlotte

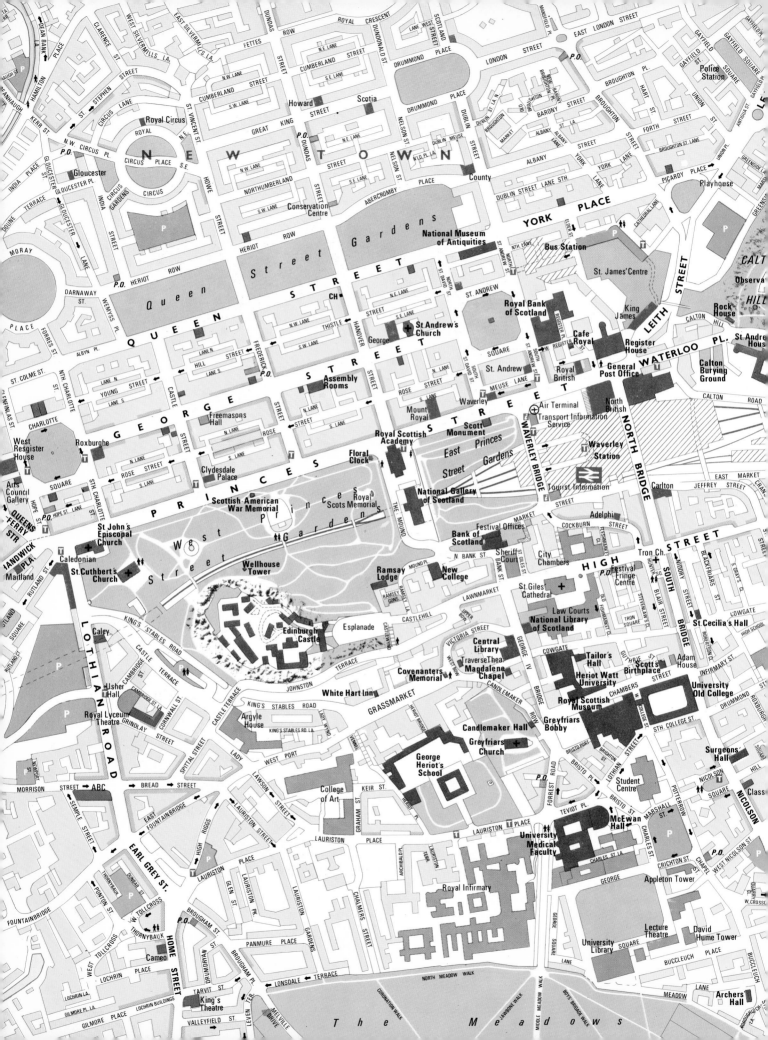

Square. One of the houses designed for the northern side of the square by Robert Adam, this classical building has been restored by the *National Trust for Scotland* as closely as possible to its original appearance, with furniture of the period. At number 6 is *Bute House*, the official residence of the Secretary of State for Scotland: at number 19 is the gallery of the *Scottish Arts Council*, where there are frequently changing exhibitions. At the turn of the 18th and 19th centuries Sir Walter Scott lived on two or three separate occasions in or near *George Street*, which runs parallel to Princes Street and, on the northern side, Queen Street, and links Charlotte Square at the west end with *St Andrews Square* at the east. At the north-east corner of St Andrews Square is the coach and bus station for the city — though the frequent conducted coach tours of the city and surrounding area — winter as well as summer — leave from the bus and coach centre at *Waverley Bridge*.

A regular City Transport sightseeing bus, summer and winter, conducts visitors around the outskirts of Edinburgh and the villages of the *Firth of Forth*. This is an interesting extension of the usual city centre sightseeing tours.

Waverley Bridge is a useful orientation point, very near the centre of the city, close to the *Scott Monument*, and well placed for the walk up the road or the footpath to the *High Street* and to the *Castle*. The main exit road from Waverley Station leads into Waverley Bridge, although people on foot can leave the station via steep flights of steps into Princes Street. This probably makes Waverley Station one of the most centrally situated railway termini in the whole of Europe.

The High Street, grand though it sounds, actually forms only a short stretch of the celebrated Royal Mile, which runs from *Castlehill* to the gates of the *Palace of Holyroodhouse*. Compared with Princes Street, in the heart of commercial Edinburgh and on the edge of the business centre, the *Royal Mile* is quiet. But at the time that the revolutionary New Town was being built, the Royal Mile would have been as noisy and dirty as any city street in Europe.

Halfway along *Lawnmarket* is a building called *Gladstone's Land*, a very good example of a 17th-century tenement building, in the care of the National Trust for Scotland: here, rich and poor lived in close, if segregated, proximity. Of the

same period is *Lady Stair's House*, now a museum containing memorabilia of R. L. Stevenson, Walter Scott and Robert Burns.

In High Street, dominating *Parliament Square*, is *St Giles' Cathedral*. This was, actually, only a cathedral for a period during the 17th century when there was a bishopric in Edinburgh. Much restored and altered, St Giles' remains *'the High Kirk o' St Giles'* — the nearest possible equivalent to a cathedral in the structure of the Church of Scotland.

John Knox the theologian and reformer, is buried in Parliament Square, next to St Giles'. His own house — or at least the building closely associated with him, because it is not certain that he actually lived there, is further down the High Street, on the opposite side of the road. Open to the public, it was built in 1473 and added to and altered in the 17th century. Behind St Giles' stands the *Parliament House*, home of Scotland's supreme court. A little further down the High Street is the new *Wax Museum*, featuring many characters and scenes from Scottish history; and at the junction of High Street with *North* and *South Bridges*, is the *Tron Church*. This is one of the places in Edinburgh where people meet to 'bring in the New Year'. Its name derives from the 17th-century 'tron' or weighing machine: if merchants whose weights were checked here were discovered to be cheats, they were, it is said, nailed up by the ears.

John Knox's House

Nearly opposite John Knox's house is the *Museum of Childhood*, one of Britain's most appealing museums, with children's toys, schoolbooks, accounts of nursery life. In Canongate, one is nearing the end of the Royal Mile. The name derives from the formal point of entry into Edinburgh for the cannons in the days of the important *Holyrood Abbey*, the remains of which are incorporated in the Palace of Holyroodhouse. This part of the city was once very fashionable and expensive to live in. In Canongate Tolbooth (1591) is housed the *City Museum* which also extends into *Huntly House*, opposite.

(From the Tolbooth Wynd — just west of Canongate Church — there is an approach path to the 19th-century *Burns Monument*).

St Giles' Cathedral

At the foot of Canongate one is close to the *Palace of Holyroodhouse*. It is the Queen's official residence in Edinburgh, and open to the public (official conducted tours only, at regular intervals, to see the *State Apartments*, the *Picture Gallery* and the *Historic Apartments*). The Picture Gallery contains the remarkable collection of paintings of 111 Scottish kings, real and legendary, painted with varying skill in record time by *Jacob de Wet*, between 1684 and 1686. Among the Historic Apartments are Mary Queen of Scots' private suite, and the audience chamber in which the first dramatic and bloody episode of Mary's life was enacted. Here her secretary and close friend Rizzio was stabbed to death.

Huntly House

South of the Royal Mile on George IV Bridge lies *Greyfriars Church* and the famous statue of *Greyfriars Bobby*, the Skye terrier which kept almost continual watch over his master's grave for fourteen years between 1848 and 1862. The church has poignant memories of the harshly imprisoned *Covenanters* who objected to restrictions imposed following the Civil War on the Scottish Church's right to choose its own ministers. The covenanters were outlawed in 1670.

Five minutes' walk east of here is the *Royal Scottish Museum* on Chambers Street. A gem of imaginative 19th-century architecture, the museum's exhibits range widely from Egyptian antiquities to natural history, to brilliant Victorian entrepreneurial technical inventions and 20th-century space exploration equipment.

If after the ascent to Edinburgh Castle (see below) and the Royal Mile the visitor has energy enough to climb *Calton Hill*

The Castle and the tall terraced houses of the Royal Mile silhouetted against the sky at the far side of Princes Street Gardens.

16

he will be rewarded by a close look at the 18th-century City Observatory Buildings, now disused, and the 'Parthenon' — the *National Monument*. This was begun in 1822 to honour the dead of the Napoleonic Wars, but the glorious and noble flourish ended in bathos when funds ran out and it was unable to be completed. It is possible to drive up Calton Hill, taking the road which runs behind the old Royal High School and site of the proposed *Scottish Assembly*.

Other places close to the centre of Edinburgh that are worth seeing are the *National Gallery of Modern Art* at *Inverleith House* in the *Royal Botanic Gardens*, the *Royal Scottish Academy* on Princes Street, where a special exhibition is normally held at the time of the *Edinburgh Festival*, and the *National Museum of Antiquities*, which concentrates on exhibits brought to the capital from Scotland's many important prehistoric sites, although also included are personal memorabilia of such figures as Robert Burns, Mary Queen of Scots and Bonnie Prince Charlie. Further afield, but worth visiting, are *Edinburgh Zoo*, four miles west, *Cramond Village*, six miles north west, *Rosslyn Chapel*, ten miles south, and *Hillend Ski Centre*, six miles south west.

Dean Village

The Castle

The silhouette of Edinburgh Castle by day or night is one of the most famous sights in Europe. A natural position of defence and a symbol of power, the volcanic rock on which the Castle stands first saw a defensive building erected in the 11th century, and it was probably defended as far back as the Iron Age. Its history has been a chequered one: in 1174 the castle was handed over to Henry II as security for the ransom of William the Lion — the first recorded occupation by the English. It was returned to the Scots in 1186, fell again into the hands of the English and was retaken by *Randolph, Earl of Moray*, nephew of Robert the Bruce, on a dark night in 1313. At the same time he destroyed all the buildings except for *St Margaret's Chapel*, dating from about 1076, and the oldest building in Edinburgh. The drama and changes of power continued until the Union of the Crowns in 1707.

The building was used and renovated by the Stuart kings, giving it a more 'modern' appearance. Today, it is used by the army.

From the Castle battlements there are good views of the city and the Firth of Forth. Among the outstanding points of interest on the tour of Edinburgh Castle that most visitors will make are: St Margaret's Chapel (see above), the *Scottish National War Memorial* (opened 1927), *Queen Mary's Rooms*, where James VI and I was born in 1566, the *Great Hall* and the *Crown Room*, which houses the *Honours of Scotland*, including the sceptre, the sword of state and the crown, remodelled in 1540 by order of James V. The crown is made of Scottish gold, ornamented with Scottish pearls and stones.

The Edinburgh International Festival

The Festival takes place normally during the last two weeks of August and the first week of September. It was inaugurated soon after the end of the last war and its prestige and following have been increasing steadily ever since. (Its full title is *The Edinburgh International Festival of Music, Drama and Art*.) *The Edinburgh Fringe* which started as an unofficial offshoot of the Festival is now in its own right the biggest arts festival in the world. The Fringe is open to any artist who can find a space to perform and its scope ranges over all the visual and performing arts.

Other attractions running concurrently with the Festival are the spectacular *Military Tattoo*, held on the Castle Esplanade, and the internationally acclaimed *Film Festival*.

The Edinburgh Tattoo, staged by searchlight on the esplanade of Edinburgh Castle, is a major attraction at Festival time.

The House of the Binns, a 15th-century fortress that was converted into a private house in the 17th century, was the first country house to be taken over by the National Trust for Scotland.

For those who are leaving Edinburgh by the *Forth Road Bridge* or on one of the main roads to the south, there are enough places of interest to make the traffic congestion that can affect most roads around the city seem tolerable. Within ten miles of the city, to the west, are the *House of the Binns*, Hopetoun House and *Linlithgow Palace*. Close to the Forth, the House of the Binns was bought in 1612 by Thomas Dalyell, a successful Scot who made good in London after the succession of James VI to the English throne (as James I). There are some elaborate ceilings and the house is famous for the fact that the *Royal Scots Greys* were raised here in 1681. The house is in the hands of the National Trust for Scotland.

Hopetoun House was begun in 1699 by Sir William Bruce (who had built the Palace of Holyroodhouse in 1696), and it was completed four years later. An extension was built in 1721 by William Adam and his famous sons, John and Robert, and their additions put the perfect finishing touches to one of the most beautiful houses in Scotland. There are views over the Forth from the landscaped gardens. The house, whose lavish interior decoration, fine furniture and great library delight thousands of visitors, is the seat of the *Marquess of Linlithgow*. Hopetoun House is west of South Queensferry, one mile north of the A904.

Linlithgow Palace juts into *Linlithgow Loch*, though the promontory on which it stands is thought to have once been an island. Its pedigree as a royal palace is almost unmatched in the whole of Scotland. Edward I, King of England, used this as his campaign headquarters against the Scots in 1301. The palace as it now stands was built for James I; James V was born here in 1512, and greatly improved and extended the building. Here, too, Mary Queen of Scots was born. The palace was much neglected during the second part of the 16th century. Charles I stayed here in 1633, the Scottish Parliament used it, as did Cromwell, Bonnie Prince Charlie and, in 1914, King George V. It is now a picturesque ruin. There are excellent views of the Palace from the M9 Edinburgh/Stirling motorway, although access is from Linlithgow itself.

Stirling

Stirling is less than an hour from Edinburgh by train or car. The new M9 motorway has put this most historic of Scottish cities well within the reach of visitors who have even an afternoon to spare from the demands of the capital. Stirling has sprawled during the last half century, but the old town,

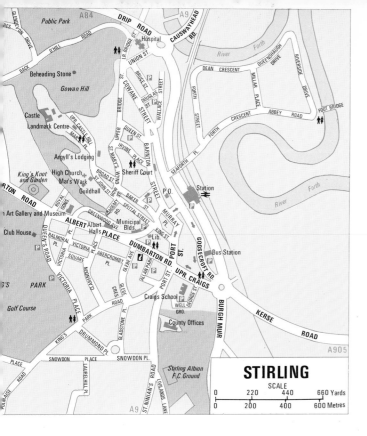

STIRLING

SCALE

| 0 | 220 | 440 | 660 Yards |
| 0 | 200 | 400 | 600 Metres |

The old bridge, Stirling

overlooked by most visitors, but, like Stirling, is a good base from which to explore *The Trossachs* and the *Queen Elizabeth Forest Park*, which lies between the tourist centre of Aberfoyle and the unspoilt eastern shores of *Loch Lomond*.

A few minutes' drive south of Stirling, off the A80, lies the Bannockburn Information Centre, commemorating the battle between the Scots and the English in 1314—a resounding victory for the Scottish army.

Doune Castle

near the castle, is well preserved. In time, the spacious, prosperous-looking Victorian buildings of the town centre will probably come in for the same amount of affection and care. The castle is superb. It was once the most important strategic fortification in Scotland, and there are magnificent views from its battlements. The castle is the regimental headquarters of the Argyll and Sutherland Highlanders, and the regimental museum contains some splendid treasures. On the castle esplanade is a statue to *Robert the Bruce*, which overlooks the distant site of the *Battle of Bannockburn*, in which Bruce defeated England's Edward II and voiced Scotland's eternal longing for independence. Close to the castle is the *Landmark Visitor Centre*, which offers similar facilities to the one at Carrbridge (see page 58). On the far side of the River Forth stands the impressive if inelegant, Wallace Monument, a tower whose 220 feet are considerably enhanced by the 360-foot Abbey Craig on which it is built. In the monument is a gallery dedicated to a number of famous Scottish figures—a bonus for the energetic visitor. At Stirling University, situated between Stirling and Bridge of Allan, on one of the most beautiful University campuses in the world, holidaymakers are able to stay during vacation times in self-contained apartments normally occupied by undergraduates. Contact the Senior Assistant Secretary, The University, Stirling.

The Victorians who made Stirling into an important commercial centre used to relax, as far as they allowed themselves, at the spa towns of Bridge of Allan and Dunblane, both just a few minutes' drive north of the town on the A9. Dunblane, whose pleasantest houses cluster round the great 13th-century cathedral, is a quiet residential town that is

Doune and Blair Drummond

Three miles west of Dunblane on the A820 lies Doune, a town once famous for its pistol manufacturers but now of considerable tourist interest because of the well-preserved 14th-century *Doune Castle*, Doune Park Gardens and *Doune Motor Museum*. Doune Castle is one of the best of its kind in Britain, and visitors get a good impression of medieval life in a castle. It was last used by Bonnie Prince Charlie to house prisoners during 1746. The castle is still the property of the Earls of Moray, to whom it came through Lord Doune, a descendant of the original owner, the Duke of Albany. The 10th Earl of Moray laid out the Doune Park Gardens in the early 19th century. There are some remarkable tall trees and, in early summer, azaleas and rhododendrons. The Motor Museum contains vehicles from Lord Doune's collection. Some of these take part in the hill climbs organised here in the early summer and in September.

Five miles north west of Stirling on the A84 lies Blair Drummond. The Victorian house is built in 'Scottish baronial' style. In the grounds is a wildlife *safari park*; where lions, giraffes, elephants, monkeys, zebras and other animals roam with considerable freedom in wide enclosures.

Gleneagles Hotel

Approximately 9 miles north of Dunblane, before the village of Auchterarder, is the hamlet of Gleneagles and, set well away from the road via a secluded drive, the *Gleneagles Hotel*. Built in 1924, this imposing hotel was the first in Britain to have a bathroom for every room. Though it is expensive (five stars) it seems less so to those guests who make use of the championship golf courses, the fishing, squash, tennis, swimming, which are part of the hotel's facilities. Though it has its critics, this internationally famous hotel is a Scottish institution.

Culross

Fife

To the east of Stirling and accessible from Edinburgh via the *Forth Road Bridge* lies the *Kingdom of Fife*, a charming part of Scotland quite unlike any other part of the country.

The ancient Kingdom has a history of great independence, and appropriately, has retained its identity even within the rather unwieldy regional structures. Fife is easily the smallest, geographically, of the Regions and, roughly covering as it does the bit of land lying between the Firth of Tay and the Firth of Forth, it is easily identifiable on any map of the country.

Approaching from Stirling, Culross (pronounced Kewross) on the coast between Kincardine and Dunfermline, is a delightful 16th- and 17th-century village which has amazingly survived almost intact, and is today owned and conserved by the National Trust for Scotland.

There was a free ferry over the narrowest part of the Firth of Forth, initiated by Queen Margaret, for 800 years before the famous *Forth Railway Bridge* was opened in 1889. The almost equally impressive road bridge was inaugurated in the 1960s.

The M90 between the Forth Bridges and Perth is one of the newest and most pleasant motorways in Britain.

Roughly equidistant between Perth and North Queensferry on the northern banks of the Firth of Forth, is Kinross, a lively little agricultural and industrial town which has, like so many places, greatly benefited from the arrival of the motorway. But the name Kinross will be less familiar to people than the name *Loch Leven*. The loch contains seven islands, and is particularly well known for the quality of its fishing and for the wildlife that settled here. It is also known as the place where Mary Queen of Scots was imprisoned in 1567, and from where she escaped — in the true tradition of historical romances — a year later. She was helped in the attempt by a friend of the young man, son of her captor, who had fallen in love with her. But her band of followers was defeated at Langside only a few days later, and she fled over the Border.

Buckie House

The coastal road between Burntisland and Leven is largely industrial but the caves near East Wemyss and West Wemyss (pronounced Weems) are interesting. The name Wemyss means 'cave' and Pittenweem derives from the same root.

Continuing along the A917 from Leven, the coastal villages become increasingly attractive. St Monans is a centre for boat-building, and Elie and Earlsferry have wide and sandy beaches ideal for children.

Pittenweem is a jewel in this pretty and historic peninsula. Hundreds of years ago an important commercial port, Pittenweem still shows signs, in its elegant harbour-side houses, of its former prosperity. It is still an important fishing town.

St Andrews

Anstruther is known locally as 'Anster'. There are good beaches, hotels, the *Scottish Fisheries Museum*, and two historic churches (Wester church and Easter church). There are boats to be hired and pleasure trips in summer to the *Isle of May*, six miles off-shore, to the south east.

Ten miles south of St Andrews is Crail, an exquisite little seaside town with a picturesque harbour. It is the most easterly of Fife's many fishing settlements, and has been well restored by the National Trust for Scotland under the *Little Houses Scheme*. This scheme has had many great successes in Fife, at Kirkcaldy, St Monans, Ceres, Falkland, Anstruther, Pittenweem and Culross.

St Andrews is the town most likely to attract visitors to this part of Scotland. It lies at the end of the A91 from Stirling, just a few miles south of Dundee across the *Tay Road Bridge*, and it is less than an hour's drive from Perth. So, in spite of St Andrews' apparent isolation it is not at all 'out on a limb'. The town got its name because relics of Andrew, one of the Apostles, were believed to have been brought here. The town is very proud of the fact that it has Scotland's oldest university (1411), the famous *Royal and Ancient Golf Club*, and the ruins of the great cathedral that was, in 1559, destroyed by a mob incited by John Knox, and then, in 1649, almost completely obliterated by Cromwellian troops who authorised the inhabitants to take the stones and use them for building. As if this were not enough, there is the remains of the 'new' castle of 1390, sandy beaches, a model village, and more.

From St Andrews, it is approximately ten miles to Cupar via the A91, but a worthwhile detour is south eastwards to Ceres, a very pretty village with a green on which celebratory games were held after the announcement of the victory over the English by *Robert the Bruce* at Bannockburn.

Cupar is a charming, busy and prosperous place in farming country. The *Thanes of Fife* lived on Castlehill. Along the narrow little alleys of the town are some tiny old houses with decorated doorways.

From Cupar, the A92 runs south westwards; in eight miles

Crail

it reaches a junction with the A912, which will bring you in three miles to Falkland, a historic and picturesque village. Falkland was designated a Conservation Area in 1970, the first such area in Scotland. *Falkland Palace* is one of the loveliest buildings in Scotland, and well worth visiting.

The Palace is owned by the Queen, though the Royal Family does not stay there. The last monarch to stay here was Charles II in 1651. The original castle dates from the 12th century, but the present building goes back to about 1450.

In the grounds is a very rare example of a royal (or 'real') tennis court of 1539. The Palace is situated, unusually, in the little town itself and, with the different architectural styles it incorporates it adds charm and grace to Falkland.

There are many other delightful little houses and 'wynds' — the alleys where tradesmen had their shops. Some buildings are owned by the National Trust for Scotland.

Rejoining the M90 motorway, access to Perth is quick and easy. North of Bridge of Earn is *Moncrieff*, a well known viewpoint, over 750 feet, overlooking the *River Tay*.

Kellie Castle

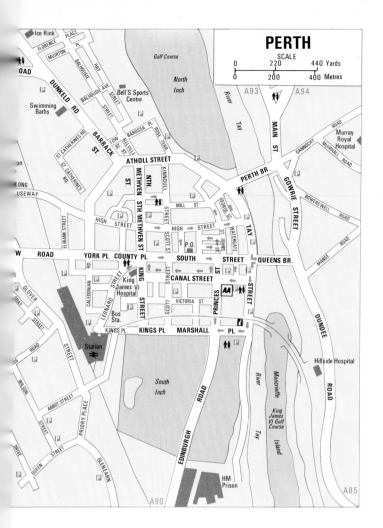

PERTH

SCALE

| 0 | 220 | 440 Yards |
| 0 | 200 | 400 Metres |

convenient for drivers approaching from the east from the coastal villages of Fife and Kinross, *Loch Leven*, Falkland and Cupar.

Even if your time for seeing Perth is limited, a visit to the audio-visual show at the Tourist Centre is a must. Housed in the former city waterworks headquarters, it is an imaginative venture.

Near Charlotte Street is the house associated with Sir Walter Scott's 'Fair Maid of Perth'. Also worth seeing are the art gallery and museum. The museum is especially good on tracing Perth's history over the last two or three hundred years. St Ninian's Cathedral is also interesting.

The *St Andrews Kirk*, although much restored, is well worth seeing. It has a famous carillon which was installed in the tower in 1936. John Buchan, the novelist and diplomat, lived in Perth, as did John Ruskin, the Victorian writer.

Perth is often called the 'gateway to the Highlands' — and with this point of departure we will leave the South East of Scotland.

Perth

Most visitors are impressed by the width of the *River Tay* as it flows through the city of Perth, with tree-lined banks, the *North* and *South Inch* parks and elegant houses on both sides of the river.

In the 13th and 14th centuries Perth (which was once known as St John's Town or St Johnstoun) was Scotland's capital city, and it was only after the death of James I in the Blackfriars monastery near here that the Royal Family moved to Edinburgh for greater safety. Perth has been an important railway junction since the middle of the 19th century, and it is much used by Motorail traffic, for the city is a very good jumping-off point for the Highlands. For travellers who make for Perth by road rather than by rail it is a very convenient first night's stop after Edinburgh, or at the end of a day's tour of Stirling, Dunblane and the *Trossachs*. It is also

South of Perth is Kinnoull Hill; on a clear day there are astonishing views of the surrounding countryside – so take your map and camera.

Hotel and Guest House Accommodation; Restaurants

Glasgow and the South West

It will come as a surprise to more adventurous visitors from outside Scotland that comparatively few Scots from the south and east of the country ever set foot on the remoter Hebridean islands. As so often happens, it is left to the outsider to discover the little-known nooks and crannies of the country, just as Englishmen are often put to shame by the knowledge that visiting Americans display of the minutiae of English history.

There are a number of beautiful islands in this south west corner of Scotland, but you cannot 'do' them quickly. The pace of life is slow, and so is the business of getting from one island to another. The character of the islands is entirely different from the mainland. They have almost completely escaped, or in some cases resisted, the worst aspects of tourist exploitation.

Each of the islands is different in character from the others, and to appreciate how some have remained completely unspoiled, try especially to see Jura and Islay (pronounced Eye-la). The deer population of Jura outnumbers humans and, even in high summer, the almost roadless island is seemingly deserted.

Islay is flatter, except for its extreme south western corner, but it has a powerful feeling of remoteness. Its west coast villages are reminiscent of the west of Ireland. There are several hotels that cater for fishermen and sportsmen, and most of these are comfortable and friendly without being pretentious. For example, there are the *Bridge* at Bridgend at the junction of the A847 and the *Port Askaig Hotel*, overlooking Jura.

On a clear day, you can see the housing estates of Ardrossan from the Isle of Arran. The eastern side of the island is like a pleasant extension of the mainland, but to travel westwards is to come into a different world. There could hardly be a greater contrast between the ferry crossings from Ardrossan to Brodick and the summer-only link between Lochranza and Claonaig, on the Kintyre Peninsula.

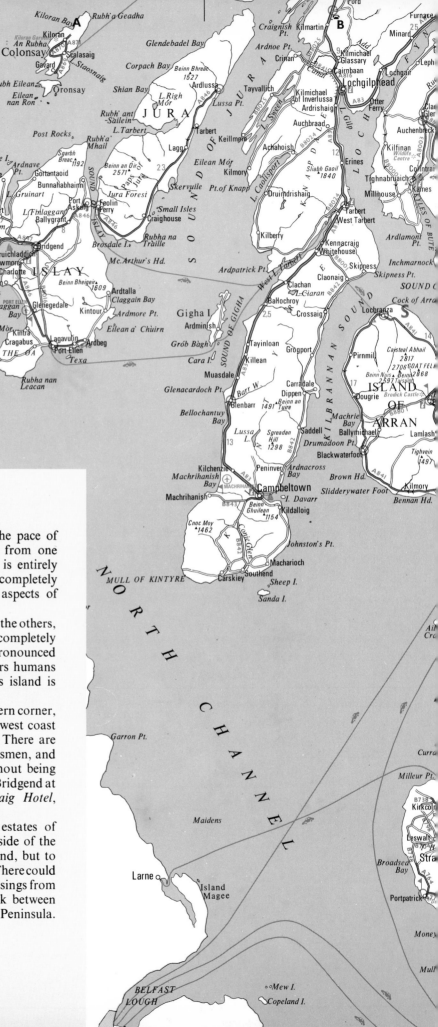

If Kintyre were an island, instead of merely almost one, it would probably be one of the most sought-after in the whole of Scotland. As it is much more prosaically a peninsula, it is little known, and, especially as you go south, quite beautiful.

Towns in this region are few, except for the comparatively populous centres of Ayr, Prestwick and the industrial towns further inland. Glasgow, of course, is Scotland's biggest city, and it has more to appeal to the casual visitor than its reputation would suggest.

At the south western and southern extremes of this region lie Dumfries and Galloway. Few visitors who are coming to Scotland for the first time visit the old county of Kirkcudbright (pronounced Kirkoobree) or even Dumfries itself. This is, however, a pleasure in store for those who have already seen the Highlands and Islands, or visitors from the south who are sensitive about the cost of petrol. This part of Scotland is, after all, much closer to the Border, and it costs less to visit. Stranraer is a departure point for ferries for Northern Ireland, but few travellers bound for Stranraer take the time to see something of the region through which the main roads pass, despite its attractiveness.

Glasgow

Glasgow is Scotland's biggest city, with a population almost twice that of Edinburgh. It is unfortunate that Glasgow is saddled with a reputation — undeserved — for being a grimy and slum-scarred remnant of the industrial revolution, for much of the city has been transformed. Glasgow has long been Scotland's commercial and industrial heart, and, as in so many great cities, its chequered and turbulent past and the tremendous energy of its citizens gives it an infectious vitality.

Glasgow is not just a glass-and-concrete 'phoenix from the ashes'. In the centre of the city many of the original 19th century buildings give the place a solid, spacious and prosperous air. There are worse ways for the first-time visitor to see Glasgow, as this writer once found, than to emerge from an overnight sleeper at Central Station and walk the couple of

Glasgow Cathedral

26

hundred yards to *George Square* to see it before the streets start to fill with people and traffic. Or one should see the place on a Sunday, when the centre is equally quiet.

In George Square there are no fewer than twelve statues to famous people whose lives have been linked with the development of Glasgow. The square is effectively the centre of the city, though that distinction has also been claimed by *Glasgow Cross*, or 'The Cross', which was once a meeting point for tradesmen and merchants. The Tolbooth was built in 1626, though the *Mercat Cross* nearby is actually a 20th-century replica.

The imposing building that takes up the whole of one side of the square is the headquarters of Glasgow District Council. *The City Chambers*, as it is known, is a symbol of the wealth and power Glasgow enjoyed during the Victorian era and it was opened by Queen Victoria herself in 1888. There are guided tours of the palatial interior.

The City Chambers, however, take second place to *Glasgow Cathedral*. Lacking the rural surroundings that set so many British cathedrals off so well, St Mungo's does not always get the attention it deserves. It is one of the most perfect examples of pre-Reformation architecture in Britain, despite the fact that after the Reformation it became, and still is, simply the Parish Church of Glasgow. Just opposite the cathedral is the oldest house in Glasgow, *Provand's Lordship*, built in 1471 for the priest in charge of St Nicholas's Hospital. It is now a museum.

Glasgow is more than just a jumping-off point for the principal holiday routes to the north and west, or to the south, depending on the direction from which one approaches the city, and it is worth taking time to see the *Art Gallery and Museum* at Kelvingrove, the *Transport Museum*, *Pollok House*, the *Botanic Gardens*, the world-famous buildings of the *Glasgow School of Art* (designed by Charles Rennie Mackintosh) and the Royal Highland Fusiliers' *Regimental Museum*. Glasgow is well endowed academically, with two universities — *Glasgow University* founded in 1451, and the newer *Strathclyde University*. Entertainment is provided by the *Citizens' Theatre* and the *King's* theatre, and the *Theatre Royal*, which is now the home of Scottish Opera. The *City Hall* is the home of the Scottish National Orchestra. Among the city's several fine hotels are the traditional North British and Central, and the modern Albany.

Of all the major cities in Britain none has roads so fast and efficient by which to effect a quick getaway as Glasgow.

The ease and speed with which the city and its suburbs can be visited without a long detour, or left behind after a visit is a source of pleasure in itself, especially for motorists making for the north bank of the Clyde or for the car-ferry points at

George Square, Glasgow. The feeling of strength and prosperity that stems from these elegant Georgian buildings matches the mood of a bright and busy modern city.

Gourock, Largs, Wemyss Bay and Ardrossan. In little more than an hour after leaving the city centre it is possible to be on a ferry bound for, say, Dunoon and the Cowal Peninsula or the pleasant and rather underestimated island of Great Cumbrae, or Arran or Bute. But in the summer months and on national holidays there can be long queues for the ferries.

If time permits there is enough to see in this corner of what is now called Strathclyde to make a couple of detours worthwhile.

The Botanic Gardens, Glasgow

Just south of Glasgow, off the A736 near Pollokshaws, *Pollok House* lies in impressive gardens and belies its nearness to the city. The 18th-century house is best known for its collection of Spanish paintings — El Greco, Murillo, Goya — and for several by William Blake.

Eaglesham is a recommended detour for drivers making for Prestwick (on the coast north of Ayr) along the A77 or the B764; it lies between Newton Mearns and East Kilbride, and a few miles to the south.

The village lies on the edge of moorland country that reaches its highest point at *Laird's Seat*. It is one of several examples in Scotland of a planned village, meant to bring prosperity to the area by setting up work for several hundred weavers. The venture, initiated by the 12th Earl of Eglington, failed, as did so many of this kind, but the village is exceptionally spacious and attractive.

En route for either Ardrossan or Largs or the small industrial town of Lochwinnoch (via the A760, off the A737) is the gateway to the *Muirshiel Country Park*, a stretch of woodland and moorland with a bird reserve, nature trails and picnic sites. There are several information centres.

Just north of Lochwinnoch, on the A737, is the *Castle Semple Water Park* which, like the Muirshiel Country Park, was set up as part of the *Clyde-Muirshiel Regional Park*. This part of the park is given over to sailing, canoeing, rowing and fishing.

The unclassified road to Muirshiel, off the B786, runs into the hills alongside the *River Calder*. The road comes to a dead end at the picnic site. The B786 continues towards Kilmacolm and joins the B761 to Port Glasgow where it then joins the A8. In Port Glasgow, a modern industrial town, is *Newark Castle* and also a replica of the steamship *Comet* built in the local

28

shipyard to commemorate the 150th anniversary of the launching of Henry Bell's original *Comet* in 1812. Continuing westwards there is the industrial town of Greenock, important for shipbuilding and sugar refineries. It also has modern container-port facilities. There is a scenic route along the Esplanade and over the Lyle Hill, where can be seen the Cross of Lorraine, built by members of the Free French Naval Forces after World War 2 to commemorate their stay in Greenock.

Just beyond Greenock the A8 connects with Gourock, with ferry connections for Dunoon. From Gourock, the A78 runs down the coast to Ayr, and even those visitors who are not planning to take a ferry from one of the ports that lie on the route of the A78, will find this a most interesting route.

Ayr is one of the most popular holiday resorts on Scotland's west coast. It is, with Alloway, closely associated with Robert Burns, Scotland's great poet. Burns was born at Alloway: from all over the world people come to see *Burns' Cottage*, now a museum. Burns' father is buried (and honoured by an expensive and quite attractive headstone) in the churchyard of the *Auldkirk* of Alloway. Also in Alloway are *Burns Monument*, the *Brig o'Doon* (made famous in 'Tam o'Shanter') and the *Land o'Burns Centre* which houses a permanent exhibition of the life and times of the poet.

There is a Burns museum, in busy Ayr High Street, at the *Tam o'Shanter Inn*. Behind the inn is the 13th-century *Auld Brig*, which was referred to in Burns' poems.

There is however, much more to Ayr than Burns. There are good beaches, shops, cinemas, theatres, golf, and the premier racecourse in Scotland.

At Prestwick, three miles north of Ayr, is Scotland's great international airport, which has a superb record of being remarkably free of fog. The town and the airport are reached from Ayr via the A77, or more directly, unless there is heavy holiday or rush hour traffic, the A79.

Just north of Prestwick there is a strange little peninsula

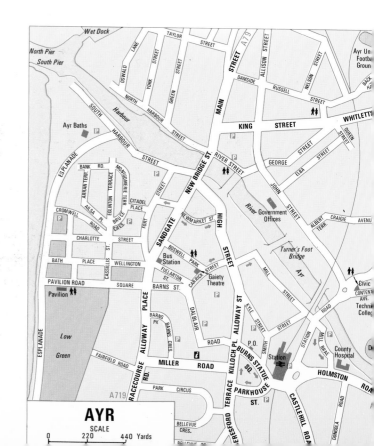

AYR

Statue to Robert Burns, Dumfries. The Burns legend adds extra appeal to a part of Scotland that is unjustly overlooked by most English visitors. But do not just be content with the legend – read at least a few of Burns' touching and lilting poems.

North of Ardrossan the scenery improves, with uninterrupted views of Arran, and beyond this, Kintyre. A recommended detour is down the curiously straight and narrow B7048, surely one of the shortest classified roads in Britain. Turn left just past Seamill — assuming you are travelling from south to north — and the road leads to the hamlet of Portencross, on a rocky coastline with superb views of Arran. The island seems close and it comes as something of a surprise to discover that it is over ten miles away at its nearest point. The narrow B7048 comes to a dead end, but there is a car park in which to turn round without difficulty.

Back on the A78, between the coast and the railway line to Largs, the smaller islands of the Firth of Clyde dominate the view to the left. Little Cumbrae, Great Cumbrae and, though it is hardly a 'small island', Bute make up this group.

Largs is a holiday resort, very much a base for trips to the islands and to Dunoon and the Cowal Peninsula. The name Largs means, simply, 'hill'. There is a famous tower monument overlooking the sea. Called *The Pencil*, it commemorates the *Battle of Largs*, 1263, when Alexander III of Scotland defeated an army from Norway, and sowed the first seeds of ultimate demise for the Vikings in the west of the country. After the battle, during which the Viking King Haakon's ships were driven ashore by high winds, the end was marked of no less than 400 years of domination by the Vikings.

The island of Great Cumbrae is popular among Scots, especially Glaswegians, but comparatively unfamiliar to other holidaymakers, except, perhaps, yachtsmen who call at Millport, the only town on the island. This resort is sheltered not only by the way it has grown up around a bay, but by the island of Bute and the all-protective Arran and Kintyre.

Wemyss Bay is six miles north of Largs. From here there are ferries to Rothesay, on Bute, and this is the departure point for Clyde cruises.

The *Isle of Bute*, and especially the resort of Rothesay, throngs in summer with holidaymakers from the cities. There is very little of the wild country of Arran and Cowal, between which Bute lies, in the whole of the island's length of roughly fifteen miles. Among the points of interest on the island are *Rothesay Castle*, open to the public, which has had as chequered a history as any on the west coast: it was taken by Norse invaders — after a struggle — and was important throughout the Stuart period; it was badly damaged in the Civil War, and restored during the 19th century by the Marquess of Bute. Just behind Rothesay Castle is the *Bute Museum*, with items of local history and archaeology.

Rothesay Castle

like a coathook on the coast, on which lies the quiet and rather 'select' seaside resort of Troon. It is best known to golfers who want to try their skill on one of five courses in the town. Troon has a sandy beach, two or three small restaurants, and a large open-air swimming pool.

Also worth a detour off the A78 is the village of Dundonald. *Dundonald Castle* stands to the right of the A759 just before the right hand turn into the village. Though much restored, this castle is remembered for being the place where Robert II and Robert III, kings of Scotland, died. Irvine is Scotland's only seaside 'new town', and boasts the *Magnum Leisure Centre*, which is on a par with the best in Europe. Saltcoats and Ardrossan are virtually one and the same place, though Saltcoats is more of a seaside resort, with the added interest for visitors of an old harbour built by the 12th Earl of Eglington — the same man who put new life into Eaglesham, the weaving village — in the early years of the 19th century. It is an increasingly important ferry port, with car ferries to Northern Ireland, the Isle of Man, and, most frequently of all, to Arran, 45 minutes away.

Arran

Even those visitors to the Ayrshire coast who never venture off-shore cannot miss the dramatic sight of the jagged peaks of Arran — an island that is at one and the same time gentle and hospitable, yet challenges even the most experienced mountain climbers and tireless hillwalkers.

Whiting Bay, on the isle of Arran. The mainland is apparently just a stone's throw away, but this spacious holiday island, which can be both wild and gentle, is well away from the bustle of everyday mainland life.

Arran is well known to golfers, for there are no fewer than seven courses, and to historians and archaeologists, for the island was always an important stopping-off place for immigrants from Europe making their way to Northern Ireland. But for thousands of ordinary holidaymakers Arran is too near the mainland to be intriguing, and too southerly to carry any Hebridean romance How much they miss . . . .

The view from *Goat Fell*, just north west of Brodick, where the Ardrossan car ferry (crossing: 45 minutes) lands, is on a fine day one of the best in Scotland. From the 2868 foot peak, easily reached by fit and well-equipped walkers, one can see the Isle of Man, the English Lakes, Islay and Jura and the Highlands. Between Brodick and the approach to Goat Fell lies *Brodick Castle*, former seat of the Dukes of Hamilton and now in the possession of the National Trust for Scotland. The Castle, which is associated with *Robert the Bruce*, who launched an assault on the mainland from here in 1306, overlooks the sandy sweep of *Brodick Bay*. There are two famous gardens: the formal garden was laid out in 1710, and the rhododendron garden in the 1920s.

There are comparatively few roads on Arran. Only two switchback roads cross the hilly central part of the island, and the coastal villages — there are no real towns — are linked by the circular A841. Visitors with little time to spare can make a round tour of Arran on this easily-negotiated, well-surfaced road that offers plenty of scenic surprises, in less than three hours. Driving south from Brodick, it is only ten minutes to the small hotels and guest-houses of *Lamlash Bay*, a quiet resort that overlooks the scree-covered Holy Island.

Near the southernmost point of Arran is *Kildonan Castle*, a ruined tower house, unfortunately unsafe for visitors. There is a cross-country road — unclassified — that links the south west of the island, via *Glen Scorrodale*, with Lamlash, but the B880, that branches off the main road at Blackwaterfoot, brings you surprisingly close to the stark black peaks of *Beinn Tarsuinn* (2706 feet) and *Beinn Nuis* (2597 feet).

North of Brodick, on a road frequented by summer visitors making for the ferry crossing at Lochranza (ferry links with Claonaig, on Kintyre, summer months only — crossing time fifteen minutes) the country is wild moorland, surprisingly reminiscent of the wilderness north of Hawick, in Border Country. There is a ruined castle at Lochranza: Robert the Bruce landed here in 1306 from Ireland, at the start of his campaign to free Scotland from the English. There is a youth hostel, for this is some of the best hill-walking country in Scotland.

The Cowal Peninsula

The ferry crossing from Gourock to Dunoon is, in summer, one of the busiest on the west coast. It takes about 30 minutes. Never is Dunoon busier than at the time of the *Cowal Highland Gathering* at the end of August. The town throngs with visitors and echoes to the sound of pipers who parade in the streets prior to the formal opening of the Gathering.

Even at that time of year, however, one quickly leaves behind the heavily populated part of the Cowal Peninsula as the road north of Dunoon, the A815, makes its way along the shores of Holy Loch and up to the *Argyll Forest Park* and *Loch Eck*. The Argyll Forest Park was the first *Forestry Commission Forest Park* to be created in Britain, in the 1930s. The needs of car-borne visitors are catered for, and there are pleasant, not too strenuous walks. There is an information centre at Kilmun on the northern shore of Holy Loch.

Three or four miles north of the head of the tranquil Loch Eck lies Strachur, on the shores of *Loch Fyne*. There is a pleasantly situated hotel, the *Creggans Inn*, just north of Strachur, also on the lochside. The B8000, which runs along the eastern side of Loch Fyne, south of Strachur, connects with Tighnabruaich, a sailing resort with a *Wildlife Centre*. The village overlooks the Isle of Bute.

Note: For Inveraray and the road to Cruachan and Oban, see West Coast.

Kintyre

Kintyre, the long spindle of hilly land that extends almost to the shores of Ireland, between the Inner Hebridean isles of Jura and Islay, and Arran, is itself almost an island. It is joined to the mainland only by the narrow neck of land by the small maritime town of Tarbert.

The name Tarbert, which appears several times on the west coast of Scotland and on the islands, comes from the Norse. It refers to the Viking theory that, if a longboat could be dragged from one shore to the next, even across land, the peninsula that was thus 'severed' was to be counted as an island. For example, the 11th-century prince, Magnus Barefoot, son of King Olaf of Norway, claimed ownership of all the Hebridean islands, and therefore he would have regarded Kintyre as a Norse protectorate.

Tarbert is a small touring centre or, at least, a stopping-off point for motorists on their way south from Oban or from the direction of Inveraray, which lies to the north east of here.

Probably even fewer motorists explore the southern part of the Kintyre peninsula than take the alternative ferry routes to Islay from West Tarbert (*Caledonian MacBrayne*) or from Kennacraig (*Western Ferries*). The Kennacraig ferry crossing, three miles further to the south of West Tarbert, arrives at Port Askaig on the north of Islay, with easy connections with Jura, while West Tarbert ferries run to Port Ellen, almost at the extreme south of Islay. The Caledonian MacBrayne ferries to Port Ellen call, on some crossings, at Gigha, a smaller island between Tayinloan on Kintyre, and Islay.

At Kennacraig the B8001 branches off the more direct A83, thus connecting with the pleasant summer-only ferry from Claonaig to Lochranza, on the Isle of Arran. From Claonaig the B842 follows a lonely and attractive course via Saddell — where there are some remains of a Cistercian monastery founded 800 years ago — to Campbeltown.

Campbeltown lost one very useful source of tourist traffic when the car ferry that connected Kintyre to Northern Ireland ceased to operate several years ago. It is still, however, an important and not unattractive fishing town — though herring catches, as everywhere, are much reduced. There are several hotels and even, at the time of writing, two cinemas.

There are whisky distilleries, which at certain times can be visited, and the natural harbour formed by *Campbeltown Loch* is a pleasant place for an afternoon or evening stroll.

The B842 links Campbeltown with Southend, a small holiday resort which is as 'away from it all' as you are ever likely to get on the Scottish mainland. There is a golf course.

From Southend an unclassified road of poor quality takes one almost to the extreme southwest point of the *Mull of Kintyre*. From here the coast of Northern Ireland and *Rathlin Island* — where Robert the Bruce is supposed to have watched the spider 'try and try again' — are clearly visible, weather permitting.

At Machrihanish, connected to Campbeltown by the B843, there are good sands for children to play on — though the shore is ribbed with menacing black rocks. There is another golf course here and, just to the north of that, the airport with connections from Glasgow: flying time about 40 minutes.

The A83 that joins Campbeltown with Tarbert and, approximately 75 miles away, Inveraray, runs close to the coast, with tantalising views of the Inner Hebridean islands of Islay, Gigha and Jura. There is a small passenger ferry between Tayinloan and the small island of Gigha (branch off the main road towards the sea, and follow the signs). The A83 is fast, straight and easy to travel.

Islay, Jura and Gigha

It takes sufficiently long to get to Islay — about three hours on the ferry, either from Kennacraig or West Tarbert — to make it seem further away than it actually is and, therefore, an even more exciting place to visit. The crossing from Kennacraig, under the auspices of Western Ferries Limited, is the more convenient for those who wish subsequently to make the five-minute crossing to Jura, which is one of the least known and possibly the most intriguing of all the Hebridean islands.

Islay is too bleak a place for many people's taste, and one's arrival at Port Ellen, a large village with something of the flavour of the west of Ireland about it, presage a somewhat dour place. The extreme south west of Islay, 'The Oa', is virtually uninhabited, and vast tracts were bought in the mid 1970s by a Dutch millionaire as a sporting estate. So lonely is Oa, in fact, that it was the centre hundreds of years ago for illicit whisky distilling, dealing and smuggling. Most visitors, however, will take the straight road past the aerodrome off Laggan Bay.

If that road, the A846, from Port Ellen via Laggan Bay, to Bowmore, seems strangely and almost unerringly straight, this is because it follows the line of a railway that was never actually built.

The countryside is flat, brown and peaty, and hauntingly beautiful.

The site of Bowmore kirk, up the hill from the quayside, is one of the most famous in Scotland. Familiar as it is, however, few people would be able to pinpoint its location. The church was built during the second half of the 19th century. It is round, local legend says, so that the devil would have no corners in which to hide. Bowmore is the unofficial capital of Islay and there are several hotels here.

Beyond Bowmore, at Bridgend (the hotel here is especially popular with fishermen) the road divides. The A846 continues along the edge of the grounds of *Islay House*, one of the very few wooded parts of the island, towards Port Askaig, the approach to Jura and the alternative ferry crossing back to

Kintyre. The A847 turns westward, out to Portnahaven, west of which there is no land until you get to Newfoundland . . . .

Whisky connoisseurs all over the world who have never been to peaty Islay will know the name well enough. For some of the finest, most distinctive-tasting malt whisky in the whole of Scotland comes from here — *Laphroaig, Bowmore, Ardbeg, Bruichladdich, Lagavulin*.

All the street names at Port Charlotte (where Bruichladdich is distilled) are in Gaelic. This village, too, with its exposed, closely-knit community, has some of the flavour of the west of Ireland.

As you stand at Port Askaig and look across to Jura, the only tarred road on that island stretches away towards high ground to the right, then disappears from view.

Jura means '*deer island*' in the old Norse tongue. The island is nearly 30 miles long, but never more than about 7 miles wide. The island's population is tiny — almost entirely centred on Craighouse, where the Jura distillery is sited.

The only road on the island, the A846, hugs the eastern edge of Jura for 23 miles — though four-wheel-drive vehicles can make further progress along a rough track some way beyond this. Just five miles south of this dead end is Tarbert — yet another example of this place-name.

Thus only a tiny part of Jura is easily accessible, so this island remains one of the most appealing of all, even to the visitor who is disinclined to stray far from his car.

There is no public transport but, in dry weather (May and June are probably the best months in which to vist Jura), this is marvellous hiking country, and bicycles are useful too. The island in the *Sound of Islay*, just off-shore from Jura itself, is *Am Fraoch Eilean*. The ruined castle that can be seen was built by the King of Argyll to guard the approach to the safe anchorage of Port Askaig on Islay.

As the road dips south and passes *Jura House*, one is close to Ardfin, where there is a famous *standing stone*, nearly 4000 years old. The original function of this is unknown, but it is known that Jura witnessed the first signs of human settlement in the whole of Scotland: flint arrowheads that are over 9000 years old have been found, well preserved by the sandy soil.

Jura has had some unlikely visitors, including George Orwell, who wrote most of the novel *1984* here; and, in 1977 the Royal Yacht Britannia was observed at anchor off the north west coast of the island.

Gigha — the name is derived from the Norse meaning 'God's island' — is accessible by passenger ferry from Tayinloan, on Kintyre, and by car ferry from West Tarbert. But since there are virtually no roads on this tiny island, there is no particular advantage in having one's car unloaded at the ferry point there. Tourist accommodation is very limited indeed, but, in good weather, it is well worth stopping off on Gigha to see the famous sub-tropical *Achamore House Gardens*.

Dumfries and Galloway

South of Ayr lie Dumfries and Galloway, and the green, low-lying 'coathook' of Scotland, the Rhins of Galloway — not well known to visitors from the south, on the whole, but seen to some extent by travellers making for Stranraer and Northern Ireland.

The A77 south of Ayr is the main road for Stranraer, and it joins the coast at Milton after following a cross-country path.

In Kirkoswald is the cottage that was inhabited by Souter Johnnie (a cobbler) in Burns' 'Tam O'Shanter', and this is open to the public as a museum.

The A719 follows the coast all the way from Ayr, and has many points of interest. Along this road lies *Newark Castle*, accessible via unclassified connecting roads from Alloway and the *Brig o'Doon* (across which Burns' Tam O'Shanter rode in the knowledge that the witches chasing him would not cross running water). Mary Queen of Scots stayed at Newark in 1563 and, seven years later, the Abbot of Crossraguel was roasted alive at *Dunure Castle* by Gilbert Kennedy, in an attempt to make him sign over the extensive and productive abbey lands. The well kept ruins of *Crossraguel Abbey* can be seen near the main road between Maybole and Kirkoswald.

Near Knoweside, three miles south of Dunure, is the famous Electric Brae, where visitors are often bemused by the apparent repeal of the laws of gravity: what appears to be the top of the hill is actually about five yards lower than the 'bottom'.

The site of Dunure on its cliff by the sea makes an aperitif on a sight-seeing trip towards the highly contrasting and much better known *Culzean Castle* (pronounced 'Cullane'). There are superb gardens that were laid out in the 1780s, and exciting views of Arran and Kintyre. There is a sophisticated visitor centre with models of the grounds and the castle (it is really a country house), and an audio-visual theatre. There are occasional lectures, and it is worth noting that children are welcome. The castle was designed for the Earl of Cassilis in the 1770s. A flat in the castle was given to Dwight Eisenhower, later President of the USA, as a tribute to his prowess as Supreme Commander of the Allied Forces during the Second World War.

From Girvan, just north of which stands Grant's Whisky Distillery, there are excursions to the strange rocky outcrop of *Ailsa Craig*, whose isolated shape dominates the horizon as one looks out to sea from near Turnberry (as it does, too, from the southern tip of the Isle of Arran).

Ailsa Craig has been called 'Paddy's Milestone', as it is halfway between Glasgow and the coast of Ireland. The rock belonged in medieval days to *Crossraguel Abbey*, being used as a place of temporary exile for troublesome or rebellious monks. It is now a bird sanctuary, whose inhabitants are hardly disturbed by the occasional summer boat from Girvan. Now protected by law, these guillemots, puffins, gannets and kittiwakes were once regarded as a great delicacy. It has been recorded that one man on a fowling expedition killed nearly 1000 puffins in one day.

Souter Johnnie's cottage, Kirkoswald. Douglas Graham and John Davidson, who became Tam o'Shanter and Souter (cobbler) Johnnie in Burns' poem 'Tam o'Shanter', are buried in Kirkoswald. There are life-size figures of characters from the poem in the garden of Davidson's former cottage.

Culzean Castle provides a perfect day's outing for all the family. It lies on the Firth of Clyde, its gardens are impressive – there is a fine 18th-century walled garden – and there are some famous interior features.

Turnberry, between Maidens and Girvan on the coast south of Culzean, is as important to the world of golf as Troon, about 25 miles to the north. The two Turnberry courses have recently been restored after being used as aerodromes. There is an outstanding hotel here, owned by British Transport Hotels several of whose hotels are in Scotland, notably at Gleneagles, Kyle of Lochalsh, Troon, Inverness and Perth. Robert the Bruce was born at *Turnberry Castle*, now a ruin.

Girvan lies not far from the extreme western edge of the *Galloway Forest Park*, which embraces the Glen Trool forest. South of Girvan, on the A77 coastal road towards Stranraer, lies Lendalfoot, a small seaside resort close to the ruined *Carleton Castle*, one of what used to be a series of watchtowers along the coast of the area called *Carrick*.

The seaside village of Ballantrae used to be a smugglers' hideout. Like so many fishing villages along the coast it is attractive enough to merit a break in one's journey. The village formed the setting for Stevenson's story, *The Master of Ballantrae*. Three miles south of Ballantrae on the A77 lie *Glenapp Castle Gardens*, open Easter to September, with extensive woodland walks, formal gardens and greenhouses. Plants and shrubs are for sale.

Just beyond Ballantrae, for the first time since leaving Ayr, the road climbs a few hundred feet, but it then drops again to *Loch Ryan*, and one's first sight of Stranraer.

Stranraer is two hours by ferry from the Irish coast at Larne, but it is a seaside holiday resort as well as a seaport. There are walks to the 400 year old castle, which is not open to the public. There is ample accommodation all year round.

A low strip of land running south and south east of Stranraer just prevents the distinctive *Rhins of Galloway* from being an island. Among the places of interest in this 'coathook' country are two gardens that lie in the southern part of the Rhins: These are the *Ardwell House Gardens* and the *Logan Botanic Gardens*. The gardens at Logan were established by two brothers, Kenneth and Douglas McDouall, last of an old family who occupied this estate since the 12th century, who spent their lives collecting plants from warmer parts of the world which they thought might survive in the comparatively mild *Mull of Galloway*. There are plants flourishing here that originally came from, for example, New Zealand, China and Tibet. *Port Logan Fishpond* at the northern end of the village is a tidal pool where cod come to be fed by hand. Open to the public Easter to September.

The A77 continues to Portpatrick, an ancient fishing

village and now a quiet holiday resort that is a good touring centre for the Rhins. Until the middle of the last century, Portpatrick was a port of embarkation for Ireland, but the harbour was very exposed to wind and weather, and began to deteriorate. There is a good beach, golf and bracing walks to, especially, *Dunskey Castle*, which dominates a headland to the south.

The lighthouse at the Mull of Galloway is open at times to the public — preferably when prior notice has been given.

No fewer than seven tides meet the extreme edge of the Mull of Galloway (the word 'Mull' denotes a headland or promontory). The Mull of Galloway figures in Robert Louis Stevenson's poem 'Heather Ale, a Galloway Legend': the legend says that the last of the Pictish kings committed suicide by jumping from one of the cliffs at the Mull, taking with him the secret recipe for heather ale.

East of Stranraer the A75 runs to Glenluce and, from here, the A747 takes one to Machars, the peninsula overlooking Wigtown Bay.

On route for Glenluce, about two miles east of Stranraer are the *Castle Kennedy Gardens*, modelled on the gardens of the Palace of Versailles in the first half of the 18th century. There is a garden centre, with unusual plants for sale, a pinetum and an avenue of tall 'monkey puzzle' trees.

Glenluce is an interesting village with the remains of *Glenluce Abbey*, two miles to the north west, the ruins of *Carscreugh Castle* (two miles to the north east), and the late 16th century country mansion of *Castle of Park*, which was built partly of stones from the ruined abbey. Walter Scott used the marriage of the daughter of the owner of Carscreugh Castle as the theme for his novel *The Bride of Lammermuir*; and *Glenluce Abbey* was the burial place of Scott's 'Young Lochinvar'.

The brightly painted houses in the seaside and farming villages of the peninsula south of Newton Stewart come as a pleasant surprise to many travellers used to the grey stone villages that are more characteristic of the west coast of Scotland.

Whithorn, which is the principal town of this region, gets its name from the *White House* or *Candida Casa* that was built by Scotland's first Christian missionary, *St Ninian*. He returned to this part of Scotland in AD 397, after making a pilgrimage to Rome — and he thus pre-dates *St Columba*, often reckoned to be the founder of Christianity in Scotland, by over 150 years.

The parish church at Whithorn was built over the remains of the priory erected by St Ninian. This, St Ninian's Kirk, now ruined, on the *Isle of Whithorn*, was the goal for pilgrims from

Glenluce Abbey, built in the 12th century, open to the public, was occupied briefly by Mary Queen of Scots in 1563. Despite its great age, some rare and beautiful architectural details are well preserved.

all over Scotland for several centuries. Robert the Bruce, James IV and Mary Queen of Scots all made the journey.

Wigtown, ten miles north of Whithorn via the A746, and the former county town of Wigtownshire, is now part of the recently established region called Dumfries and Galloway. Wigtown is small and unspoilt, with some evidence of its considerable former importance. There are good walks to the edge of the river estuary (where two Covenanter martyrs, Margaret McLauchlan and Margaret Wilson were tied to a stake in 1685 and allowed to drown) and excursions to the *Kilsture Forest*, four miles south via the A746. Three miles to the west, just off the B733, are the *Standing Stones of Torhouse*, a Bronze Age monument of nineteen stones forming a circle reminiscent of the Stone Ring at Avebury, in Wiltshire.

Newton Stewart is a major junction of the A714 road from Girvan to Wigtown, the A75 from Stranraer to Dumfries and the A712 from New Galloway, which joins the A75 just to the east of the town. This busy market town, in which a comfortable hotel and a focus for much local life is the *Galloway Arms*, is a convenient touring centre, especially for visitors who want to penetrate the Galloway Forest Park, formerly known as the *Glen Trool Forest Park*. There is good salmon fishing in the area. The *Galloway Forest Park* takes in several of the highest peaks of southern Scotland, as well as no fewer than seven forests. Ten peaks in the park are higher than 2000 feet. The heart of the park, in which it is possible to see red deer and golden eagles, is near *Loch Trool*, 11 miles from Newton Stewart, and there is holiday accommodation in the forestry village of Glentrool. Some of the wildest parts of the park can be seen from the A712 New Galloway road, but the park is always best enjoyed by walkers who can leave the road behind.

Detailed maps of the area are available from newsagents, bookshops and general stores in Newton Stewart, New Galloway and elsewhere.

Robert the Bruce is known to have taken refuge in this part of Galloway, and its wild and remote beauty will surprise visitors who expect this part of Scotland to be featureless. This south western corner of Scotland is growing in importance as a tourist area, for it is more readily accessible to visitors from over the border than the better known but still distant Highlands.

The A75 from Newton Stewart to Gatehouse of Fleet passes along the north east corner of Wigtown Bay through Creetown, very close to *Barholm Castle*. The fiery preacher John Knox once stayed here.

Burns is said to have composed the famous *Scots Wha Ha'e* in the *Murray Arms*, in Gatehouse of Fleet. This Bannockburn rallying call is often mentioned in guide books but rarely is any part of it quoted:

'Scots, wha ha'e wi' Wallace bled
Scots, wham Bruce has aften led
Welcome to your gory bed
Or to victorie.'

The small town of Gatehouse of Fleet is pleasantly situated among low hills, and the surrounding woods enhance its attraction.

The detour off the A75 Dumfries road to Kirkcudbright is worthwhile. In the *Tolbooth*, at one end of the wide High Street, John Paul Jones, a founder of the American navy, was imprisoned: Jones was born near here in 1747. A natural adventurer, and a seaman, he was charged with murder, but eventually was released. Disgruntled, to say the least, he joined the American side during the War of Independence and returned to *St Mary's Isle* (actually a peninsula) in Kirkcudbright Bay in an attempt to capture the Earl of Selkirk.

The Tolbooth, Kirkcudbright

Burns is credited with having penned yet another poem — the Selkirk Grace — in a local hostelry, the *Selkirk Arms*:

'Some hae meat and canna eat
And some wad eat that want it;
But we hae meat and we can eat,
Sae let the Lord be thankit.'

Near the seafront is *MacLellan's Castle*, built in the 1580s by Sir Thomas MacLellan with stones from the ruined priory. North of Kirkcudbright is Tongland, with a great hydro-electric power station (open to the public from the end of June to mid September — book beforehand), and north east of there, along the A711, are *Threave Gardens* and *Threave Castle*. They are not adjacent, but are about two miles apart, on opposite sides of the road. Threave Gardens, just south of the A711, are open all year round (the house is not open to the public) and incorporate a School of Gardening. In spring the gardens are outstanding for their daffodils, in May and June for their rhododendrons, in July and August for roses, and even in the autumn the pleasure of the place is not diminished, for then the herbaceous plants and rock gardens come into their own. Threave Castle is most romantically sited. It was erected by the third earl of Douglas, and the unscrupulous 'Black Douglasses' maintained the castle as their stronghold for over a hundred years. The castle housed French prisoners during the Napoleonic Wars at the beginning of the 19th century.

Loch Trool lies in the heart of the Galloway Forest Park. Robert the Bruce hid from the English among the woods that now, as they did hundreds of years ago, add extra colour to the landscape.

Threave is virtually on the outskirts of Castle Douglas, a market town and shopping centre. Dumfries is only seventeen miles from here.

Threave Castle

Ten minutes' drive east of Kirkcudbright on the A711 is *Dundrennan Abbey*. Mary Queen of Scots spent her last night in Scotland here before her troops were defeated at the *Battle of Langside*. Immediately after her defeat she fled to England by sea from what is now known as Port Mary, two miles due south of here.

The A711 continues to Dumfries, via Dalbeattie, which in the 19th century was an important and prosperous granite-producing town. An agreeable detour is via the A710 around Criffell (1868 feet) to *Sweetheart Abbey*. This romantic name comes from the story of the loving devotion of Devorguila, wife of John de Baliol, who founded Balliol College, in Oxford and mother of John de Baliol, who became King of Scotland. She had his heart embalmed when he died, and ordered it to be interred with her in the chapel of the New Abbey — as Sweetheart Abbey is officially called — when she died. Her death came twenty years later. From here it is five miles to Dumfries.

Dumfries

Dumfries is an important place historically and strategically. Its records go back nearly 800 years. The name is believed to derive from *Drum Phreas*, which means 'the fort in the wood'. Dumfries's former importance as a seaport has long passed, though the river Nith is still wide and deep. Robert Burns lived here between 1791 and his death in 1796, and here he wrote over 100 poems. The *Globe Inn* remains today, and contains Burns' favourite chair. There is a statue to the poet near *Greyfriars Church*, close to the most elegant part of the town. *Burns' House* is now a museum. In the churchyard of *St Michael's* is the elaborate *Burns Tomb*, a Grecian Mausoleum to which Burns' body was removed in 1819, 23 years after his death.

The six-arched bridge over the River Nith is part 15th century. There were originally nine arches on the bridge, which replaced a wooden one built by the Lady Devorguila (see above).

J. M. Barrie, creator of Peter Pan, attended the grammar school at Dumfries — known now as Dumfries Academy. This is a town of great interest, though it is generally neglected by English visitors. It is well worth a couple of nights' stop and is justifiably called Queen of the South.

Although it lies ten miles west of the vital A74 trunk road from Carlisle to Glasgow, Dumfries is the meeting point of six major roads linking parts of the south of Scotland.

Carlyle's birthplace, Ecclefechan

The main road between Glasgow and Carlisle is the A74 (part of the route being the M74) which runs close to Lanark and even closer to Moffat. The latter is a pleasant touring centre for the eastern side of the Border Country (see page 12).

The Lanark area, though neglected by most visitors, is of considerable interest.

Lanark's name lives on in the oldest horse-racing trophy in the country — the *Lanark Silver Bell*, which was presented to the town by William the Lion. But if racegoers no longer converge on Lanark, this is still a busy market town (market day is Monday): and every year, at the beginning of June, *Lanimer Day* is held. Traditional ceremonies are performed in the streets, as well as the important Border/Lowland one of 'Riding the Marches', also known elsewhere as 'beating the bounds', that is, checking that the boundaries of the parish have not been eroded during the previous year.

(The road through the old mining settlement of Leadhills, westwards from the A74 north of Moffat, brings one into the pre-1975 county of Lanarkshire. This part of Scotland lying so close to the amorphous, though not altogether unpleasant suburbs of Glasgow, links Dumfries and the coast at Ayr and Prestwick.)

Less than two miles south of Lanark, at the end of an unclassified road, lies New Lanark, a rare and well-preserved example of an 18th century planned community, an embodiment of enlightened, if paternalistic, ideas that came from wealthy industrialists. Here, in 1784, David Dale, a Glasgow businessman and banker, and Richard Arkwright, the industrialist and pioneer of cotton-spinning by modern methods, built mills. Alongside these there grew up comparatively healthy tenement blocks with a modicum of 'mod cons'. Many of the original buildings remain.

Biggar, less than ten miles from Lanark, via the A73 and then the A72, is not much visited by outsiders, but it is one of the pleasantest small towns in the south of Scotland. The family of *William Ewart Gladstone*, one of the most remarkable British Prime Ministers of the last 150 years (and *bête noir* of Queen Victoria) hailed from Biggar. In the town is the *Gladstone Court Museum*, one of several largely unsung municipal museums of Britain, within whose walls are recreated the life and times of previous centuries — here, by means of an old cobbler's shop, an early telephone exchange, a chemist's shop with pestles and mortars and even a large earthenware jar marked 'leeches'.

Bothwell Castle

At the extreme north eastern point of *Strathclyde Park*, 1600 acres of countryside that provide a breathing space for people living in an industrial part of the country, lies Bothwell, which is the largest stone castle in Scotland and now a rather picturesque ruin. Its history is closely linked with the Scottish struggle for independence. It was an important English base in the west of Scotland for much of its existence.

North of Glasgow

Drivers more used to the tedium of negotiating English cities such as Manchester and London will find that Glasgow presents few problems. New by-passes and sensible traffic schemes means that it is easy for Glaswegians to take advantage of their geographical position, only about 25 or 30 miles from some of Scotland's most peaceful scenery.

It is as easy to reach the north bank of the Clyde, near Dumbarton as it is to get on the A74 or M74. Just four or five minutes north of Dumbarton, on the A82, one gets one's first glimpse of *Loch Lomond*. The drawback, of course, of the easy accessibility of such a famous place is that the road can become a nose-to-tail column of cars.

The A82 for some way beyond Dumbarton, however, is a dual carriageway.

Past the junction with the B832 Helensburgh road the country becomes less open and the road hugs the lochside with hills to the west. Well worth a stop, when the house is open, is *Rossdhu*, lying right by the Loch. It is the family seat of the Colquhouns. Though only a limited number of rooms are open to the public, there are some very interesting heirlooms, and pleasant gardens.

Several of Loch Lomond's 30 islands lie between Rossdhu and Luss. They form an unusually well-protected nature reserve.

Loch Lomond, the largest stretch of land-locked water in Britain, suffers from its popularity only a little, for it is easy to get away on foot from the road to the water's edge. As the loch narrows and the road approaches Tarbet the scenery on the eastern side becomes more dramatic.

Note: the northern part of Loch Lomond falls into the West Coast Section.

Hotel and Guest House Accommodation

Johnston & Bacon

Publishers of maps and Scottish books since 1825

The Clans, Septs and Regiments of the Scottish Highlands

By Frank Adam
Eighth edition, revised by Sir Thomas Innes of Learney

An encyclopaedia of Highland clanship, covering the history astructure of the clan system, Celtic culture, the Highland regiments, clan insignia and Scottish heraldry 'A wonderful work of reference' — **The Coat of Arms**

632 pages, fully illustrated, including colour, 216 x 140mm, ISBN 0 7179 4500 6, £7.75.

The Tartans of the Clans and Families of Scotland

By Sir Thomas Innes of Learney
Eighth Edition

This classic work has 114 pages of colour photographs of tartans for both Lowland and Highland families. Each tartan is accompanied by a history of the clan or family concerned, together with the chief's coat of arms, the badge, and the slogan. In his introduction, the author explains the clan system from the legal, social, and historical points of view. 'This will continue to be the standard work on the Scottish clans and tartans for a long time to come' — **The Genealogical Quarterly**

300 pages, fully illustrated in colour and line, 216 x 140mm, ISBN 0 7179 4501 4, £5.75

The Scottish Clans and their Tartans

This ever-popular book is now in its 42nd edition, and enhanced with 96 full-colour plates of tartans photographed from the actual cloth. A history of the clan accompanies each tartan.
'The Bible of the tartan' — **The Scots Magazine**

272 pages, 96 full-colour illustrations, 140 x 121mm, ISBN 0 7179 4504 9, £1.35

The Scottish Tartans

Revised by Sir Thomas Innes of Learney

This comprehensive guide to Scottish tartans and clans has been continuously in print for over 60 years. It includes histories of the clans and alongside these coloured illustrations of the tartans and their wearers, of plant badges and of coats of arms.

112 pages, illustrated in colour, 152 x 152mm, hardboard, ISBN 0 7179 4502 2, £1.75; tartan bound, ISBN 0 7179 4503 0, £3.75.

Johnston & Bacon Publishers,
Tanfield House, Tanfield Lane, Edinburgh EH3 5LL
a division of Cassell Ltd, 35 Red Lion Square, London WC1R 4SG

The West Coast

For the purposes of this guide the West Coast embraces, as well as Oban, Mull, and the peninsulas of Ardnamurchan and Morvern, much of the country through which visitors will pass on the main westerly route towards Loch Ness: places like the gentle *Trossachs*, the glowering *Glen Coe* (the name means 'Vale of Tears'), the mighty *Ben Nevis*, the important Highland crossroads at Fort William, and the best known Scottish loch of them all, *Loch Ness*.

This part of Scotland has crowded roads in summer, and a tendency towards commercial 'tartanry', souvenir booths, and craft shops which is more marked than in other areas of Scotland. The A82, which passes alongside *Loch Lomond* and through *Glen Coe* towards Inverness, is an important trunk road, and a vital link to the north to the isolated beauty spots of the far north west coast. Nor is this part of Scotland neglected by coach tour operators, and names such as *Rannoch Moor*, *Spean Bridge* and *Fort Augustus* are as familiar to tourists from the south of England as Watford Gap or Gatwick Airport. On this road, at Ballachulish, there was until recently a famous ferry, which has now been replaced — to most drivers' relief — by a bridge which cuts an hour off the journey time. The scenic route through Kinlochleven which was used as an alternative to waiting for the ferry does, of course, still exist.

In this section also are the northerly part of the *Kintyre peninsula*; two out of Scotland's three great *Forest Parks*, set up after the last war; and the westerly part of the great region called Tayside, which was set up after local government reorganisation in spring 1975.

This section takes in, too, the whole of the great *Caledonian Canal* which, by incorporating man-made waterways and natural lochs, cuts right across Scotland from Fort William to Inverness. It was built in the very early 19th century, in an attempt to overcome the problems involved in circumnavigating the North of Scotland, with its notoriously dangerous currents and storms.

The stretch of road between the northern end of Loch Lomond and Oban, another of the 'Highland crossroads', is one of the busiest during the holiday season, but there are ways to escape traffic fumes and still make progress, if that is one's intention, to the west coast. Seeing Oban is almost mandatory: this is a lively port and holiday town with ferry connections to several Hebridean islands, including the Isle of Mull — almost as accessible as Skye and, some maintain, more appealing to the visitor.

Proximity to the mainland certainly does not diminish an island's appeal: Skye, for one, is little more than a stone's throw from the railway station at Lochalsh, but you could hardly find a more romantic and self-contained place, and

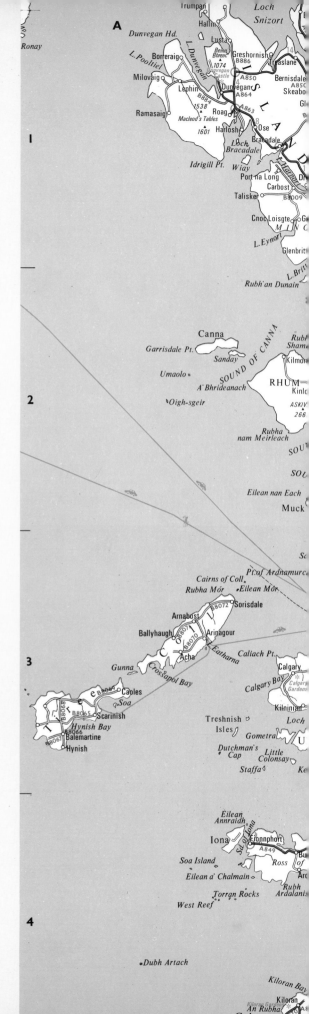

Mull, so close to the bustling and much-visited town of Oban, is hauntingly different from the rest of the Inner Hebrides and the mainland. For very many visitors, in fact, Mull is the essence of Western Scotland — there are beautiful beaches and picturesque little roads, and wild, peaty moors and high hills, whose passes in bad weather can be awesome and inhospitable. But when the sun is warm and visibility is good, you wonder if you will ever be able to bring yourself to leave.

Mallaig, just beyond the westernmost point of *Loch Morar*, may be less visited than Oban or Kyle of Lochalsh. This route, nicknamed 'The Road to the Isles', tends to be neglected by travellers with little time to linger, but it is a most interesting part of the coast.

The Trossachs

The Trossachs is a very distinctive and easily defined part of central Scotland that has been called 'Scotland in Miniature'. It is popular with coach tour operators, embracing as it does *Loch Katrine*, Aberfoyle, much of the *Queen Elizabeth Forest Park*, the eastern shores of *Loch Lomond* and the spectacular minor road, the B829 — known as *Duke's Pass* — from Aberfoyle to Inversnaid, via *Loch Arklet*. This road figures in many guides to Scotland for cyclists, and walkers too will find its fifteen miles extremely attractive, especially beyond Loch Arklet.

Inversnaid is at the western edge of the Queen Elizabeth Forest Park, on the pleasant wooded eastern shores of Loch Lomond. There are impressive views of the peaks of *Ben Vorlich* (3088 feet), *Ben Vane* (3044 feet) and *Ben Arthur* (2891 feet). Ben Arthur is known as 'The Cobbler', from the similarity to the Gaelic name for the mountain to the word 'cobbler'. Hikers can make their way by a track to the north end of Loch Lomond and then walk the eastern shore down to the *Trossachs Gorge* which lies between Loch Katrine and *Loch Achray*.

From low-lying Aberfoyle the road climbs gently to a point at which it is about mid-way between two of the highest peaks in central Scotland — *Ben Lomond* (3194 feet) and *Ben Venue* (2386 feet). Aberfoyle is a holiday resort quite suitable for visitors without their own transport, for there are well-organised Forestry Commission walks fanning out into the surrounding hills, and access within a two-hour walk to six or seven lochs, including *Lake of Menteith* (the only 'loch' in Scotland to be called a lake). On Inchmahome Island in the Lake of Menteith are the attractive ruins of the 13th- and 14th-century *Inchmahome Priory*, which may be visited at certain times by taking the ferry from nearby Port of Menteith.

The Trossachs, whose name means 'bristling country', is well wooded, with glens that are easy on the eye, not oppressive, with many lochs and lochans (small lochs). It is said that Sir Walter Scott was the first to 'discover' the region, and it figures as the setting for his *Rob Roy* and *Lady of the Lake*. The Lake poets, Wordsworth and Coleridge, found here a natural dramatic setting that surpassed even the Lake District.

The Trossachs region is taken to extend as far eastwards as Callander, one of several gateways to the Highlands; it is a well laid out and spacious town with some elegant houses. Callander was the inspiration for Tannochbrae, in television's *Dr Finlay's Casebook*. The A84, which runs north of Stirling as far as Lochearnhead, passes through the town, and, just north of Callander, runs through the *Pass of Leny*. Beyond here, one reaches *Loch Lubnaig* and descends towards *Strathyre*, then gets one's first sight, to the east, of *Loch Earn*. Salmon breed in Loch Lubnaig, and it is possible during the autumn to see them leap the *Falls of Leny*, where the *River Leny* tumbles dramatically on its southward course.

Lochearnhead is a busy tourist centre in the summer. This, too, is good walking country. South of the village, which is known as a waterskiing and sailing centre, is *Edinample Castle*, on the shores of *Loch Earn*. Built in 1630, it is a local landmark, and looks very attractive against the hills to the south of the loch. It is not open to the public.

There are impressive views from the highest point of the A85 road, at *Glen Ogle*, running from Lochearnhead to *Glen Dochart*. Killin, a small tourist resort, is perhaps best known for the *Falls of Dochart*, a series of rapids spanned by an ancient bridge. On one of the islands in the river is the burial place of the Clan McNab, an important local family who left the area in the early 19th century.

The A827 links Killin and Kenmore, and runs alongside *Loch Tay* through the village of Lawers, at the foot of *Ben Lawers* (3984 feet). Close to Lawers there are signs to the National Trust for Scotland's *Mountain Visitor Centre*, on the southern slopes of Ben Lawers. The site was bought by the Trust not just for its great beauty but because of the exceptional range of arctic–alpine flora existing here.

Inveraray, Oban

On the southern edge of this West Coast region runs the A83 Arrochar to Campbeltown road (which is comparatively little-known along its southern half beyond Lochgilphead). At the eastern extreme of the A83 lies the village of Tarbet, on Loch Lomond. Here, the A82 runs south to Glasgow.

Inveraray (west of Tarbet on the A83) is a pleasantly situated small holiday resort. Surrounded by woods that are cool in summer and protective in winter this was, during the 17th century, one of the most important townships on the western side of Scotland. In 1692, at the time of the massacre at Glen Coe, the Chief of the Clan MacDonald was imprisoned in the town jail for cattle stealing and suspected murder: but he escaped, and it was considered too dangerous to pursue him back to Glen Coe.

The tumbling Falls of Dochart at Killin – a place of beauty at all times of the year.

Kilchurn Castle

The present town was laid out in the 18th century, when the Duke of Argyll built *Inveraray Castle* and pulled down most of what was left of the old village. The castle itself suffered a disastrous fire in 1975 that almost destroyed both the exterior and the interior and burnt many of the castle's greatest treasures. Enormous efforts have been made to restore it, and it is once again open to the public, and still contains many family heirlooms. Among the historical records there is, for example, Rob Roy's sporran! The castle is an essential stopping point for travellers who find themselves in this part of Scotland.

North of Inveraray the A819, a comparatively quiet switchback road through *Glen Aray*, approaches the head of *Loch Awe* within fifteen miles. At the northern extreme of Loch Awe lies *Kilchurn Castle* on an island in the Loch. It is a most romantically-ruined relic of the original castle, which was built in 1440. The top of one of the towers was blown down in the great gale of 1879 that also destroyed the *Tay Bridge*.

Just west of the junction of the A819 and the A85 lies the massive *Cruachan Power Station*, where there is a popular visitors' centre, with easy access. Of all the hydro-electric schemes in Scotland, this is the most impressive. The power house of the great dam lies literally inside the 3689-foot high *Ben Cruachan*. Visitors can take a minibus two-thirds of a mile into the heart of the great mountain to see the scheme functioning. From Ben Cruachan it is an easy ten-mile drive via Taynuilt, where there is a good hotel, and via the western extreme of *Loch Etive*, to Oban.

Oban is an important touring and holiday centre. Several ferry routes have their embarkation point here, including those to Mull, Coll, Tiree, Barra, Colonsay and South Uist — as well, incidentally, as St Kilda (though scheduled ferries do not run to that remote island).

At times, when the weather is right, as on a calm and cloudless summer evening — the sea-front at Oban, with its substantial two and three star hotels looking across the narrow *Sound of Kerrera* could almost be a prosperous and fashionable Black Sea resort — not quite the Riviera, but still heady and invigorating.

The story of *McCaig's Tower*, as distinctive a landmark as any on the west coast, is worth repeating. Erected between 1897 and 1902 by a rich banker, it was never completed. The tower (often referred to as McCaig's Folly) stands on *Battery Hill*, overlooking the harbour. It is best seen from the water. John Stuart McCaig's intention was, ostensibly, to provide employment for stonemasons in and around Oban.

Oban has a cinema and flourishing live entertainment in the summer months. The town is the railhead for the line from the rail junction at Crianlarich, and is accessible in about four hours from Glasgow.

Oban to Tarbert

The A816 south of Oban is a switchback road with some fine views that, after 16 miles, gives way at Lochgilphead to the A83. The A83 begins its meanderings near Arrochar, skirts the northern and western edges of *Loch Fyne* and then runs to the far south of the Kintyre peninsula. Beyond Lochgilphead the road to Kintyre is straight and fast, even when it is busy with holiday traffic.

South of Tarbert, however, the holiday traffic peters out noticeably, even at peak times. Some drivers make for the car-ferry terminals at West Loch Tarbert and Kennacraig (for Jura, Gigha and Islay). Others branch off at Kennacraig to the B8001 for the summer ferry service from Claonaig to Lochranza on the Isle of Arran — but not many make it to Campbeltown.

Though the drive from Tarbert to Campbeltown can be easily accomplished in two hours, the scenery can still be enjoyed with just a little time extra. The A816 between Oban and Lochgilphead, however, requires more time if the road is to be enjoyed — and a whole day or more if the by-roads and then the B roads to Seil or Crinan or the attractive lochs of *Nell*, *Avich*, and *Craignish* are to be explored. The cluster of islands reached by the B844 makes good day excursion country for the thousands of visitors who come to this part of Scotland. The picturesque high–arched bridge to Seil Island is known as the 'Bridge across the Atlantic'. There are passenger ferries to the small island of Easdale and car ferries to *Luing*. There are summer boat trips from Cuan to several of the Inner Hebridean islands, including a trip that runs close to the famous *Corryvreckan Whirlpool* between Scarba and Jura, where George Orwell (who wrote part of his novel *1984* on Jura) nearly drowned.

Coll and Tiree

The passenger ferry that links Oban, on the mainland, and Tobermory, on Mull, also plies between Tobermory and the islands of Coll and Tiree. They are geographically one island, only separated from each other by a two-mile strait. It is,

The Falls of Avich, Loch Avich. Approached by an unclassified road running east of Kilmelford, this charming spot repays the effort of the easy walk to it.

however, a notoriously rough stretch of water — too rough for any ferry to negotiate on a regular basis. So travelling from Coll to Tiree involves a ferry trip of about 20 miles. Both islands are famous for their beaches and their summertime profusion of wild flowers.

Coll is quieter than Tiree, with a population of under 200. Most people live in or near the village of Arinangour, from where bicycles may be hired. But a car is a worthwile proposition, as there are over 20 miles of roads, and is especially useful if one is going on to Tiree.

Tiree has nearly five times the population of Coll. It is low-lying, fertile, but not entirely flat. There is golfing here, an airport, and — as on Coll — a number of secluded, sandy bays. The island is well known for one thing particularly — there are no rabbits: and the local crofters benefit accordingly. The name of the island comes from the Gaelic *tir eth* meaning 'land of corn'. The only real centre of population is Scarinish, where there are several guest houses. Camping is permitted and enjoyable on both Coll and Tiree, but prospective campers should choose their sites with care, as these low-lying islands are notoriously windy.

Colonsay and Oronsay

Colonsay and Oronsay are really one island, though they are only linked at low tide. There is a golf course and a hotel, several fertile farms, and at *Colonsay House*, are the fine sub-tropical *Kiloran Gardens*, open to the public.

At no point are Colonsay and Oronsay more than three miles wide. The islands are ideal for walkers, especially if they make it to the top of *Carnan Eoin* for views from Iona to the *Paps of Jura*. Oronsay, indeed, might have become more significant a place in the history of Christianity in Britain than Iona, except for the fact that St Columba vowed not to establish his mission in sight of Ireland — and, in certain conditions, Ireland *is* visible from Oronsay.

Rhum, Eigg, Muck and Canna

Of the four strange islands that make up that part of the Inner Hebrides known as the Small Isles, only two, Eigg and Canna have accommodation. Camping is, however, allowed on Rhum. On the fourth island, Muck, there are no permanent facilities for overnight visitors — although holiday cottages are sometimes available.

There are boats (passengers only) four times a week from Mallaig, calling at Eigg, Rhum and Canna, and, less frequently, at Muck (private boats can also be hired from Eigg to Muck).

Muck, Eigg and Canna are fertile, hilly islands, inhabited by only a handful of farming families. Rhum is more mountainous, with three peaks of about 2500 feet, plus several lesser ones, in its twenty square miles.

Eigg, nearest to the mainland (approximately seven miles) and first point of call on the round trip from Mallaig to the islands, does have an independent passenger ferry to the mainland, and even an aerodrome. The name of the island

comes from the noticeable gap in the hilly skyline when one sees the island from afar: '*Eilean Eige*' means 'island of the notch'. The most dramatic part of Eigg is the *An Sgurr*, a weirdly-shaped mass of volcanic rock reminiscent, when viewed from the island's only landing point at Galmisdale, of Suilven, in Sutherland.

Muck, three miles southwest of Eigg, is easily the smallest of this self-contained, independent-minded and fascinating quartet. Its name derives from *Muic*, or sow. There are approximately 25 people living on this island — a comparatively high population, for Eigg — a much larger place — only has 40 or so. There is lobster fishing on the island which, like Eigg and Canna, is privately owned. The nearest mainland point to Muck is *Sanna Point*, on Ardnamurchan.

Rhum is not privately owned, but in the hands of the Nature Conservancy Council. *Kinloch Castle*, an unlikely Edwardian sandstone castellated house, is the headquarters of the Nature Conservancy Council on the island. It is open at times to the public. There are nature trails, and camping is permitted, but hill climbing can be dangerous and solitary hikers are not permitted. There are golden eagles to be seen among the high peaks and red deer are studied and carefully culled each year to maintain a stable population.

The island of Canna is linked to yet another small island, Sanday, by a footbridge. Low lying and fertile, these two are idyllic in warm weather, and there are superb views of the *Cuillins*, on Skye, and the peaks of Rhum. The island is privately owned by a farmer who, as well as breeding cattle and sheep, has turned Canna into something of a wildlife preserve. Camping and some accommodation are available on the island.

Mull

Skye has a hold on the popular imagination. It *is* a romantic island with its comparatively strong Gaelic tradition and its world-famous *Cuillins*. But Mull, which is similar in some respects (for example, easy access from the mainland, with no great feeling of isolation, much wild and lonely mountainous country, and a tremendous variety of scenery) has a great many devotees, among them people who already know Skye.

Mull is only about 25 miles across, but its coast is so remarkably ravaged by the sea that its perimeter is nearly 300 miles long. Leaving the ferry point at Craignure (access from Oban 45 minutes, approximately), the road is well-surfaced and surprisingly fast. *Duart Castle*, the ancestral home of the Macleans of Duart, is open to the public. The castle is clearly visible from the sea approach to Craignure from Oban but not from the road. Close to Duart there are attractive glimpses of *Loch Spelve*, in soft woodland country. But soon after this comes the pass through dramatic *Glen More*, to the south of

The harbour of Tobermory, the only town on Mull, is charming and colourful. It is much used by ferries, fishing boats and pleasure craft.

Duart Castle

the highest peak on Mull, *Ben More*. This is craggy, seemingly remote country, especially in bad weather. The main road, the A849, passes through Bunessan, a small resort, to the south of which are fine sandy and rocky beaches. The road continues to Fionnphort (pronounced Finnafort), where there is access to the passenger ferry for Iona — though a car ferry terminal is, at the time of writing, being constructed.

Drivers on Mull coming south west from Craignure who do not want to continue to Fionnphort and Bunessan should turn northwards onto the B8035 coastal road. This leads to Salen, via *Loch na Keal* past some spectacular coastline scenery. *MacKinnon's Cave*, accessible from Balmeanach at low tide, is well worth a visit. At Salen the B8035 joins the main road from Craignure to Tobermory. An interesting alternative road, if time is available, is the B8073 to Tobermory, a slightly longer route which runs towards Calgary and Dervaig. Calgary gave its name to Calgary in Canada because of the number of emigrants to the New World from here.

Dervaig has a claim to fame, too, because it is the home of a tiny theatre, the *Mull Little Theatre*, manned by just two people: it is certainly the smallest theatre in the world run on a professional basis.

Tobermory is often associated in people's minds with the Spanish treasure ship that is known to lie about 150 feet offshore in Tobermory Bay. The ship was a galleon from the Spanish Armada which was driven into the shelter of Tobermory Bay in 1588 during a gale. According to contemporary reports, although the Spaniards were well received, fed and made to feel at home, it seemed as if they were about to set sail without paying for the hospitality they had been given. One islander, Donald Maclean, went aboard to enforce payment, but was arrested. He managed to escape, and in revenge set fire to the ship, which sank. (For those considering looking for the treasure, it is believed to lie now under a considerable quantity of silt.)

Tobermory is one of the most attractive towns in the Highlands and Islands, and has adequate holiday accom-

modation. The harbour is sheltered, and there is usually a lot of coming and going of yachts, fishing boats and cargo vessels.

Iona

Iona is where Columba, in AD 563, arrived from Ireland with twelve companions, and began the process of spreading a Celtic version of Christianity throughout the islands of the west coast and gradually over the mainland of Scotland, and then the rest of Britain. It was because of this, allied to the fact that Iona had been a religious centre for hundreds of years beforehand (Druidic customs, for example, blended with Christianity here) that kings from many parts of northern Europe were brought here to be buried. Forty-eight Scottish kings, four Irish kings, and seven kings of Norway were interred on Iona.

No trace of the original monastery remains, but a cathedral building restored between 1902 and 1910 is visited by pilgrims from all over the world. What the cathedral on Iona lacks in physical beauty it makes up for with historical associations. Apart from the cathedral, other places worth seeing on the island are the *Hermit's Cell* and *Reilig Odhrain* ('the burial place of the kings'). There are also two smaller churches and a distinctive 15th-century cross almost thirteen feet high.

Staffa

From Oban and Mull there are boat excursions to romantic Staffa. In the right weather conditions, landing is possible, but the views from the excursion launch are impressive enough, even if it proves impossible to land. The most famous of Staffa's sea-ravaged and awe-inspiring caverns is *Fingal's Cave*, immortalised by Mendelssohn.

Staffa

Fort William

Ben Nevis and Glen Coe

Back on the mainland, Fort William is a civilised springboard to some of the wildest and most inhospitable country in Scotland. There is a large number of hotels, including some new ones (always a sign of present and anticipated prosperity); a *Tourist Information Centre* with an astonishing range of literature, including guide books, maps, and topographical surveys; a *Museum of Highland Life*; and a *Scottish Crafts Centre*, open between Easter and October, where the high-quality goods on display are generally for sale. There is a cinema, a number of opportunities — again in season — to enjoy folk music and perhaps somewhat tourist-orientated *ceilidhs*, and several good shops selling authentic Scottish woollens.

Fort William owes its importance as a town largely to its geographical location. The fort was built by the English in 1755 as one of a series of forts (Fort William, Fort Augustus, Fort George) used as military bases to control the Highlands. Today its geographical situation makes it a major 'Highlands crossroads', and of great importance to Scotland's tourist industry.

Ben Nevis, at 4406 feet the highest mountain not only in Scotland but in Great Britain, lies only five miles to the south east: an unclassified road towards Polldubh brings one through part of *Glen Nevis* towards 'the Ben'. Ben Nevis is easily climbed in good weather by a 'tourist' track from the Fort William side, but as with all Scottish mountains, proper clothing should always be worn. A race up Ben Nevis is held annually from the Post Office in Fort William and back, and unbelievably short times are achieved. It must be one of the toughest runs in the world.

Loch Linnhe, which Fort William overlooks, is a sea loch: it becomes the *Firth of Lorn* between Mull and the railhead of Oban. The Glasgow–Mallaig railway, whose most scenic stretch begins at Fort William, links the town indirectly (via the Mallaig/Armadale ferry) with Skye, and thus the Western Isles.

Glen Coe and the wild *Rannoch Moor*, two of Britain's wildernesses lie to the south of Fort William. The *Massacre of Glencoe* took place on 13 February 1692, against the background of Highlanders' unwillingness to accept William III as king. One by one the clans swore the oath of allegiance, but it was the MacDonalds of Glencoe who held back longest. Though it seems that the clan chief was actually in time, having trekked to Inveraray to sign the oath, it was — though details are difficult to come by — apparently decided to make an example of the diehards. Soldiers, including many Campbells (a degree of enmity exists between the clans even today) were billeted on the MacDonalds in an apparently friendly routine camp, and these troops turned on their hosts early on the morning of the 13th. Of the 200 or so inhabitants, about a quarter were killed outright, and many others died of exposure and wounds as they wandered alone and friendless among the moors.

Beyond Glen Coe, the A82 runs through Tyndrum (a convenient stopping place with craft shops, cafes and hotels) and Ardlui, where a friendly hotel stands by the shores of *Loch Lomond*, with gardens extending right down to the famous Loch: the A82 continues south ultimately to Dumbarton and Glasgow.

Ardgour to Ardnamurchan, Morvern and Mallaig

For those visitors to Fort William who take the three-minute ferry crossing from just north of Onich to Corran in Ardgour, or who travel instead via the A830 and the head of *Loch Eil*, and back on the A861 along the west bank of *Loch Linnhe* to Ardgour, there opens up a little known part of Scotland that always seems much more cut off than it actually is. Like Kintyre, it is a peninsula that is sufficiently remote and little-visited to seem more like an island.

Both Morvern and Ardnamurchan, which make up the irregularly shaped mass of land on either side of *Loch Sunart*, have limited accommodation, but it is well worth the effort to seek out a small hotel or guesthouse in order to enjoy a part of Scotland that is closer than one would realise to the busy main holiday routes south of Fort William.

Of the two regions, Morvern is slightly better known because of the car-ferry connection from Lochaline to Fishnish on Mull (although most holidaymakers are unaware of this crossing, which is a shorter and cheaper route to the Isle of Mull than the 45 minute crossing from Oban to Craignure). For those who do make use of this ferry, petrol costs do not compare unfavourably, especially if, from Mull, one wishes ultimately to get to Ardgour, Ballachulish, Glencoe or Fort William.

At Strontian, where the roads for Lochaline and Ardnamurchan diverge, and where there is a *Nature Conservancy Council Nature Trail*, one gets one's first glimpse of the narrow, boomerang-shaped *Loch Sunart*. Here, the road to Lochaline becomes the A884.

Lochaline, the ferry-point, has a couple of small shops and a filling station. High-grade sand for use in the manufacture of top quality glass for scientific purposes is produced here, but Lochaline, happily, is still nothing more than a small village.

The *Ardnamurchan Peninsula* has its narrowest point near Salen. Here the main A861 road strikes northwards towards Mallaig. Drivers bound for Ardnamurchan should follow the B8007 to Glen Borrodale. The hotel here is a spectacular building that had an uncertain future until it was taken over in the mid 1970s by Trust Houses Forte. From here there is an extremely tortuous and narrow road to the only township of any size on the peninsula, Kilchoan.

There are two or three small hotels here, good hill walking and fishing for brown trout in several lochs and lochans. There is a ferry — passengers only — to Tobermory, on Mull. The road continues to Achosnich, from where it is possible to reach *Ardnamurchan Point*, where stands the westernmost lighthouse on the mainland of the United Kingdom.

North of Salen, for travellers making for Mallaig, the A861 is somewhat faster than the Glen Borrodale/Kilchoan road,

Loch Sunart, from near Strontian. Visitors who make for the Lochaline to Fishnish ferry to Mull will pass this way, through varied and beautiful coastline and moorland scenery.

though there are so many tempting viewpoints that progress may be slow. At Kinlochmoidart, a few miles beyond the extreme southwestern end of the narrow *Loch Shiel*, there is a row of seven beech trees that are said to commemorate the seven men of Moidart — the name given to this region. These seven men landed with Bonnie Prince Charlie in 1745 on his way to raise the standard at Glenfinnan. A monument commemorating this event stands on the main A830 road between Arisaig and Fort William.

At Lochailort, the A861 joins both the Fort William road, the A830, and the picturesque Mallaig railway. Road and rail run more or less together (from Mallaig to the middle of Glen Spean, a distance of about 45 miles).

On the '*Road to the Isles*', as this route round *Loch Morar* is often called, there are good views of the Inner Hebrides,

especially Rhum, Eigg and Muck. This is Jacobite country: Bonnie Prince Charlie landed here in his abortive attempt to seize the crown in 1745, and it was from here that, just over a year later, he escaped, his attempted coup a shambles.

In good weather the views from the sea-road around Loch Morar are more reminiscent of a Caribbean island than of Scotland. For here are the famous *Morar White Sands*, with clear, turquoise-green water that (until the temperature is actually tested) always seems very inviting.

Loch Morar is the deepest loch in Scotland, and probably in Europe: it is over 1000 feet deep. It is also a rival to Loch Ness in that there is supposed to be a monster lurking in its dark recesses. Less fantastic are the salmon and sea trout that are caught here by anglers.

Mallaig is a ferry terminal for boats to Skye (half-hour crossings to near Armadale, and for the small Hebridean isles of Rhum, Eigg, Muck and Canna). In spite of a general decline in herring fishing and severe government restrictions imposed during the late 1970s, Mallaig remains an important fishing town. The harbour is always busy and it is a great source of interest to visitors staying in one of the small hotels and guesthouses here.

Within walking distance from Mallaig, there are outstanding scenic views from *Mallaigmore* and — after a more demanding hike — from *Carn a' Ghobhair*. There are also very enjoyable boat trips to be taken to *Loch Nevis* and

Were it not for the A82, which strikes through its black heart, Glen Coe would remain a secret to all but the most enterprising traveller. It is more grim than beautiful, bleak, treeless, awe-inspiring.

round the *Knoydart* peninsula to *Loch Hourn*.

Mallaig is both the end of the road (A830) and the end of the line: the outstandingly pretty rail trip that begins in Glasgow, taking about six hours, reaches its end and its climax here. Enterprising visitors will use Mallaig as a starting point for visits to the Hebridean islands and to Skye, but for those who cannot, and wish to return towards Fort William and the A9, the A830 is for the most part fast and well-surfaced and there are several points of interest.

The road runs along the southern edge of what, even in Highland terms, is a barren and inhospitable range of hills with many peaks over 3000 feet high, and with very few access roads.

The monument at Glenfinnan

Loch Shiel, whose northern end is graced by the famous *Glenfinnan Monument*, is almost eighteen miles long, stretching southwest between high rocky banks. During the holiday season there are boat cruises on the loch.

The Glenfinnan Monument was erected in 1815 to commemorate the Jacobite rising of 1745 by a descendant of Prince Charles Edward Stuart's most loyal followers. It is enhanced by a visitor centre; here one can follow Charles's progress after the standard was raised at Glenfinnan — where morale was never higher.

W. Douglas Simpson, in his book *The Highlands of Scotland* remembers how Queen Victoria described her visit to Loch Shiel in 1873, when she was aged 54: '... I thought I never saw a lovelier or more romantic site, or one which told its history so well. What a scene it must have been in 1745! and here was I the descendant of the Stuarts, and of the very king whom Prince Charles sought to overthrow, sitting and walking about privately and peaceably.'

Details of the summer boat trips on Loch Shiel can be had from the *Loch Shiel Hotel* at Acharacle, at the far end of the loch.

During the summer months and at public holiday times traffic between Glenfinnan and Fort William, now only sixteen miles to the east, can be heavy. For the last few miles of the route the road runs alongside *Loch Eil*.

Travelling towards Fort William from the west, or from the road on the far side of Loch Linnhe, one appreciates how much Fort William is dominated by the massive bulk of Ben Nevis.

North to Inverness

Loch Ness, Fort Augustus, Glen Moriston

The *Caledonian Canal* begins just north of Fort William, flanked in its early stages by the B8004 which, however, veers eastwards when the canal reaches *Loch Lochy*. The canal links Loch Linnhe, on which Fort William stands, and the *Moray Firth*, about 55 miles away to the north east — and more than two-thirds of this great slice through the Highlands is natural, not man-made. The canal's great commercial importance faded during the latter part of the 19th century, but holiday cruisers use it more and more: it has become one of the great leisure attractions of modern-day Scotland.

The A82 north of *Spean Bridge* runs along the eastern shore of *Loch Lochy*, then sidesteps to the west of *Loch Oich* before it passes through the village of Invergarry. There are two comfortable hotels here, the *Glengarry Castle*, and the smaller, quieter *Invergarry*.

A diversion — to Kyle of Lochalsh

The A87 runs north west from Invergarry towards *Glen Shiel*, *Loch Duich*, past *Eilean Donan Castle*, and thus to within a stone's throw of the Isle of Skye at *Kyle of Lochalsh*. In the summer months the road is busy with holiday traffic, but it is one of the most impressive of Highland routes and never difficult for drivers to negotiate. In busy times when it is tempting to get away from the stream of traffic, there are several possible detours along lonely roads that climb into the hills.

The estates of *Kintail* and *Glomach* are the property of the National Trust for Scotland. Heady and varied countryside this, including beautiful glens and stretches of water, and the mountains known as the 'Five Sisters of Kintail'. There is a National Trust camping site near the head of *Loch Duich*, and a Visitor Centre with information about the Kintail Estate. Even this great estate is just a tiny part of the vast, under-populated lands to the north of the A87. About five miles north east of Morvich are the famous *Falls of Glomach*: a sight accorded, however, only to the hardy walker, for there is a difficult three-mile hike across open moorland when the rough road from Morvich peters out.

If the Falls of Glomach are visited by comparatively few people, the castle of *Eilean Donan*, just east of Dornie, is one of the most photographed and visited landmarks in the Highlands. Accessible by a picturesque causeway, Eilean Donan had a chequered history until 1719, when it was virtually destroyed during a Jacobite rebellion. It was rebuilt at immense cost, with several of the original remains incorporated, early this century. It is open to the public.

Kyle of Lochalsh is just nine miles due west, and the open vista of Lochalsh that greets motorists is a pleasant relief for the eye after the mountainous passes through the hills from Morvich.

Between Invergarry and Fort Augustus the man-made Caledonian Canal links *Loch Oich* and *Loch Ness*, and there are seven locks in this stretch of the canal. Fort Augustus was one of a chain of forts of strategic importance on the military road built by General Wade in about 1725 as part of the English Government's attempts to subdue the restless Highlanders. In 1867, Fort Augustus was sold to Lord Lovat, and his son later presented it to the English *Order of St Benedict*. Part of the original buildings are incorporated into the 19th-century abbey here — an interesting example of 19th-century ecclesiastical architecture, and now a Roman Catholic boys' school.

There is in the town a *Great Glen Exhibition*, which depicts the character of the area in its displays, and includes a section on the Loch Ness Monster. Loch Ness itself is some 24 miles long, and in places, over 774 feet deep. Recent sonar probings indicate depths of up to 1000 feet. The A82 runs along the western edge of the Loch, doubles inwards to Invermoriston and then out again, then almost dead straight towards Drumnadrochit and then again quite straight to Inverness. The road is well surfaced and well maintained but it can also be very dangerous because of the hundreds of thousands of visitors who come here every year, and who tend to drive with a weather-eye open for the Monster. In places the road is dramatically close to both the water and the mountain side.

The A82 makes a westerly loop towards Drumnadrochit, a touring centre with several hotels, none of them more spacious or beautifully situated than *Polmaly House*, near the eastern edge of *Glen Urquhart*. On a headland in Loch Ness stands *Castle Urquhart*, once one of the biggest and most important castles in Scotland. Even in its ruined state it is impressive as it juts into Loch Ness. It belongs to the Department of the Environment, and is open to the public.

Drumnadrochit is deservedly a popular holiday centre, hardly more than a village. It is perfectly placed for excursions into the beautiful and remote country of *Glen Affric*, *Glen Cannich* and *Strathglass*. There are hydro-electric schemes, but they have been as sympathetically landscaped as possible. There is an easily negotiated round trip from Drumnadrochit, via the A831, to Beauly, there to join the A9, by which one can drive eastwards to Inverness or northwards towards the *Black Isle* and the *Cromarty Firth*. As another alternative, branch off on to the A832 at Muir of Ord for the far north west.

Illustrated maps from
Johnston & Bacon

The Visitor's Map of Scotland

An ideal memento of a Scottish holiday. This magnificent full-colour pictorial map shows counties, roads, and major towns; the coats of arms of 36 towns and cities; 62 colour photographs of well-known places and spectacular views; and examples of fine Celtic jewelry.

1010 x 760mm, paper folded in card cover, ISBN 07179 4554 5, 50p; paper, rolled, with hangers for wall display. ISBN 0 7179 4555 3, £1.00

Clan Map of the Scottish Highlands

A coloured map of Scotland showing the clan district and surrounded by eighteen figures in ancient and modern Highland dress. Also shown are sixty-five tartans with the chief's arms where applicable, and the arms and flag of Scotland.

1010 x 760mm, paper folded in card cover, ISBN 0 7179 4509 X, 55p

The Facts about Loch Ness and The Monster

Compiled by Tim Dinsdale

Here are displayed the beauty and mystery of this world-famous Highland loch. Illustrations of the highlights of the hunt for the 'Loch Ness Monster', together with charts, diagrams, facts and figures, make this an informative and decorative map. The colour centre-piece, 26 inches long, gives a 3-dimensional non-perspective bird's eye view of the loch, its immediate mountainous surroundings, and underwater topography.

Map-folded, 890 x 660mm, ISBN 0 7179 4227 9, 95p

Edinburgh Castle: an illustrated history

by J B Barclay

A decorative souvenir and a fascinating historical guide. The centre feature is a bird's eye veiw of the castle, esplanade and the castle slopes as seen from the north-east. There are twenty colour drawings of exteriors and interiors of the Castle's buildings, and 24 illustrations of heraldic arms, historical figures and architectural details.

Map-folded 890 x 660mm, ISBN 0 7179 4229 5, 95p

The Abbey and Palace of Holyrood House

by J. B. Barclay

A decorative souvenir and historical guide with 34 colour drawings.

660 x 890mm, Folded as map, 0 7179 4241 4. Rolled, 0 7179 4240 6, 95p.

Stirling Castle

by J. B. Barclay

A decorative souvenir and historical guide with 31 colour drawings.

660 x 890mm. Folded as map, 0 7179 4233 5. Rolled, 0 7179 4234 6, 95p.

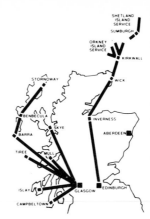

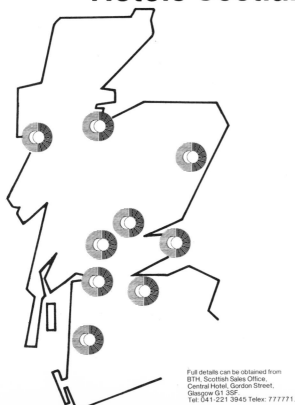

The North East

Parts of this area are well on the tourist beat. Speyside, Royal Deeside and much of Tayside around Perth, Loch Tay and Dunkeld is postcard and calendar country. But it is probably only whisky connoisseurs who get to know the country just to the south of the Moray Firth, where the peaty streams that feed the River Spey provide water for some of the best whisky in the world, and only those visitors who like to get well off the beaten track stop off to see the busy fishing ports of Fraserburgh or Peterhead. For every ten holidaymakers who travel along the spectacular A93 between Aberdeen and Braemar, probably only one sees anything of the coastal strip between Aberdeen and Dundee. But it will repay the effort: Stonehaven, Dunnottar, Edzell, Brechin — all of these are places to gladden the heart of the man who is tired of souvenir shops and caravan trailers, for none of them are ever overrun with holidaymakers. Only Carnoustie, about half an hour's drive north east of Dundee, gets a lot of attention, on account of its world famous championship golf courses — but golfers get to see a lot of Scotland that non-golfers overlook. It is a very good argument for taking up the game.

In spite of Queen Victoria's excursions into the Spey Valley, courtesy of the railway that thrust towards the very heart of the Cairngorms, it is Deeside that enjoys the appellation 'Royal'. Touristic honours are evenly divided, however, between the two regions. Both have the resorts and the facilities for a fortnight's holiday without the need to stray far from the rivers that run through them, though Speyside has established a reputation for being an all-year-round playground that effectively satisfies the holiday needs of both outdoor sportsmen and young children. The hotel and sports centre developments at Aviemore and Carrbridge met with opposition when they were first built, but they have had no adverse effect on the surrounding countryside, unless ski lifts and runs or the sight of lines of pony-trekkers on the horizon is deemed to be an adverse effect.

The driver who joins the A93 near Blairgowrie, 16 miles north of Perth, and stays on it all the way to Ballater could, even if he goes nowhere else, claim to have seen something of the best of the Highlands. It is one of the two or three finest trunk roads in Britain. The A9 north of Perth, towards Dunkeld and Pitlochry, is hardly less impressive, even if it is faster and carries more heavy lorries. It links some of Scotland's most attractive small towns.

If it appears that the area that we have designated 'the North East' is varied, even all-embracing, that is underlined by the fact that Tayside, most of which falls into our North East section, has been judged by international tourist organisations to have 38 out of the 39 natural advantages a

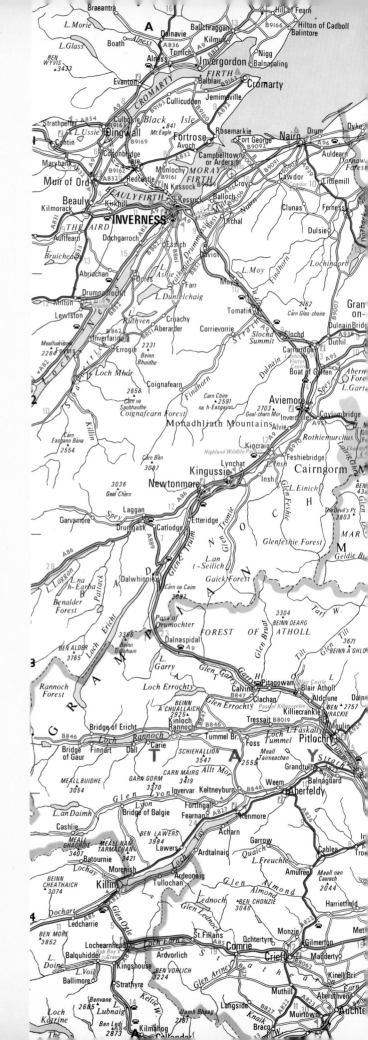

Glamis Castle

tourist-orientated area could have — the exception being that it has no habitable islands.

The 120-mile long River Tay and its more important tributaries, the Tummel and the Earn, are fed by Highland streams and lochs that support some of the fattest and best salmon, brown trout and rainbow trout in the world. One such tributary is the River Isla, into which in turn, feeds Dean Water. On Dean Water lies *Glamis Castle*; home of the Earls of Strathmore and birthplace of Princess Margaret, it is one of the most romantic castles in Scotland. Since it is one of the most visited tourist landmarks, it helps to bring a number of people into the underrated east of the region.

Comrie, Crieff

and the Sma' Glen

The great east–west trunk route, the A85, begins in Dundee and ends in Oban. This road links Lochearnhead with Perth and passes through the pretty village of St Fillans (at the eastern end of Loch Earn), Comrie and Crieff. In the loch near St Fillans is *Neish Isle*, a place of refuge for the Clan Neish, inveterate enemies of the MacNabs.

The name Comrie means 'confluence of streams'. It is a popular holiday centre with several hotels, including *The Royal*, visited by Queen Victoria in the company of John Brown, and by Lloyd George. There are pleasant walks to the waterfalls at *Glen Turret*, and to *Glen Lednock* and the famous *Devil's Cauldron*. The village is also known for the occasional earth tremors it experiences, for it lies on the Highland Fault that divides the Highlands from the Lowlands.

From the *Knock of Crieff* (nearly 1000 feet) to the north of Crieff, there are fine views of the surrounding area. The town was destroyed, during the 1715 uprising, by Jacobites, but was extensively rebuilt during the first half of the 18th century. Most of the houses in its steep streets formed part of a plan, and this Highland gateway is a pleasant place to stop. There is ample accommodation, usually even at the height of the season, with half a dozen starred hotels and a number of small and unpretentious hotels and guest houses.

From Crieff it is approximately twelve miles to Perth.

The alternative routes from Crieff to Dunkeld or Aberfeldy via the A822, which winds through the *Sma' Glen*, are both worth exploring. And from the delightful tiny village of Amulree, an unclassified road runs westwards past *Loch Freuchie*. It is now possible to drive with comfort over the gated road along *Glen Quaich* to Kenmore. There are spectacular views in both directions from the high points of this road.

Glen Lyon, Aberfeldy

and Loch Tay

Follow the unclassified road running north from the Mountain Visitor Centre at *Ben Lawers*. It runs over bleak but magnificent high mountain moorland towards *Glen Lyon*. Glen Lyon is a high-lying, remote but accessible, region of lochs and lochans, rushing streams and rivers, and several hydro-electric installations. It is the longest and one of the most beautiful glens in Scotland. The road through it runs eastward towards the pretty village of Fortingall, where there is a yew-tree said to be over 3000 years old. The road beyond here joins the B846, then continues east towards Aberfeldy (also accessible from Killin via the A827).

Aberfeldy saw, in 1733, the first-ever bridge over the River Tay. It was built by General Wade as part of the complex of military roads by which he intended to subjugate the unruly Scots, and the bridge still stands.

Wade built nearly 300 miles of roads in Scotland after the rebellion of 1715 and, at Weem, on the B846, he is commemorated by an inn sign.

The castle just to the south east of Weem was built in 1570 by the chief of the Menzies clans, who, with the MacGregors and Robertsons, virtually dominated Glen Lyon and much of the country around.

At Aberfeldy there is a striking memorial to the Black Watch, which was absorbed into the British Army in 1740: the Black Watch, originally a 'watch' of clan chiefs keen to maintain some semblance of law and order among the glens, got their name from the sombre black and green tartan they

The Wade Bridge, Aberfeldy

adopted in order to be distinguished from the English redcoats, or 'red soldiers'.

From Aberfeldy there are two routes to Dunkeld: via the A826, then the A822, through high and lonely country, or via Strath Tay, along the A827 and then the A9. Along this low-lying road lies Grandtully, where the *National Canoeing Championships* are held each summer. *Grandtully Castle* has been in the hands of the same family, the Stewarts of Grandtully, for nearly 600 years.

At Logierait, just before the junction with the A9, and the confluence of the Tay and the Tummel, Rob Roy was imprisoned in 1717. This part of Scotland, as a glance at the map will suggest, is very suitable for not-too-strenuous holiday touring. There is a lot to be seen in a round trip of between 40 and 80 miles, and there is a sufficient number of minor, largely deserted, unclassified roads to make a trip into the hills of special interest.

Stirling (see page 19) and Perth (see page 23), though busy towns with a certain amount of industry, have not been unduly spoilt, and they make good bases for touring the ancient kingdom of Fife, the *Trossachs*, the *Ochil Hills* — much, in fact, of that part of the country uninspiringly called *Central Region*.

Dundee to Aviemore

Dundee is typical of those cities around Britain that have had their history and their charm overshadowed by heavy industry and a somewhat grimy image. Among the things Dundee is traditionally associated with are thick-cut marmalade, the uncanny number of journalists it has exported all over the world, and the versifier William McGonagall, 'the world's worst poet', who wrote about, among other things, the Tay railway bridge:

'Beautiful new railway bridge of the Silvery Tay
 With thy beautiful side screens along your railway
 Which will be a great protection on a windy day
 So the railway carriages won't be blown away.'

Dundee has character and is worth a couple of hours at least of one's time. The River Tay is wide, about two miles wide at this point, and it is worth crossing by road or rail just for the pleasure of it. From the *Law Hill* there is a fine panorama in all directions — east along the Firth of Tay and the Angus coast, south over the bridges to Fife and west over the Carse of Gowrie and the Sidlaw Hills to the Grampians.

From Dundee it is only a short step to the Highlands, far removed though the city may at first seem to be from there. To get to Dunkeld, take the A923 northwest of Dundee. The approach to this lovely little town, through wooded glens, signals the approach to wilder and more interesting country. Dunkeld has a cathedral, with a well-preserved cathedral precinct, and has a fine situation on the fast-flowing River Tay. This is a good stopping-off point for overnight or longer. The A9 to Pitlochry runs along the River Tay for much of its route, but the road leaves the Tay and joins the Tummel for the last few miles.

Pitlochry is a busy touring and holiday centre with, probably, more hotels than any other Scottish resort of roughly comparable size. At the time of writing the *Pitlochry Festival Theatre* is planning to build new premises for its

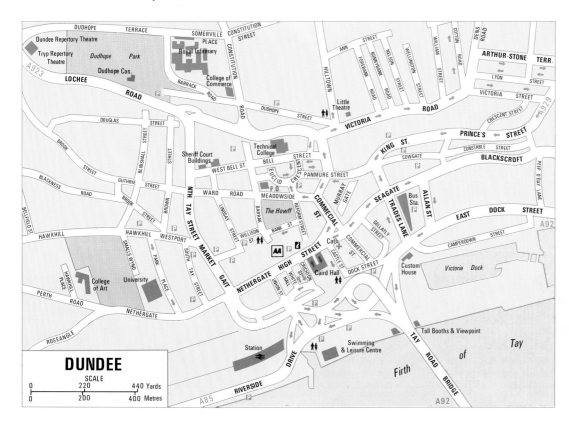

prestigious summer season. The town also has a cinema and a celebrated fish-ladder incorporated in the huge Pitlochry dam — which is worth a visit for its own sake.

Connoisseurs of wild countryside will do well to branch westwards, north of Pitlochry, along the B8019 which runs past *Loch Tummel* and the spectacular *Queen's View*, through Kinloch Rannoch and along *Loch Rannoch* itself towards Rannoch station. The road comes to a dead end at Rannoch station, but it is possible to pick up a train here for Fort William and thence to Mallaig. Remember to check the railway timetables.

Eastwards from Pitlochry, the A924 strikes quickly into the high-lying southerly foothills of the *Grampians* that divide *Strathtay* and the A9 from *Glen Shee* and the approach, via Braemar to *Royal Deeside*.

Back on the A9, the village of Blair Atholl is best known for *Blair Castle*, seat of the Duke of Atholl. The castle figured in the 1745 uprising, and has been very effectively restored over the centuries. Blair Atholl is reached from Pitlochry via the famous *Pass of Killiecrankie*, where there was a great Jacobite victory in 1689 against the troops of William III. There are impressive wooded banks surrounding the pass, and delightful walks along the *River Garry*.

The A9 north of Blair Atholl runs through the southerly part of the *Forest of Atholl*. But, as strangers will discover elsewhere, the word 'forest' in the Highlands usually denotes a barren moorland waste, not trees and thick woods.

North of *Glen Garry* the road, which continues to accompany the single track railway, reaches the *Pass of Drumochter*, the highest point anywhere in Britain reached by railway.

It was no mean feat of engineering, and the roadbuilders, too, are commemorated in a stone beside the road which marks the spot where the navvies from Dunkeld met those coming south from Inverness.

The country here is exceptionally lonely and bleak, mostly to be enjoyed from the comfort of a car. It is something of a relief to begin the descent from *Glen Truim*, towards *Upper Strath Spey*. Here the countryside becomes wooded and more fertile.

Close to the junction of the A9 with the A86 lies Newtonmore, a Cairngorms skiing resort and a good touring centre for the mountains. It is the most southerly of the Speyside holiday towns, with hotels, good opportunities for pony-trekking — usually available to complete beginners — and, of special interest to hundreds of thousands of people around the world, the *Clan Macpherson Museum*. The clan holds an annual rally here, and the *Newtonmore Highland Games* are held here every August.

Kingussie is just three miles to the north of Newtonmore. There is a golf course here, and the town is also a skiing resort. The *Highland Folk Museum* (it is sometimes known as *Am Fasgadh* or The Shelter) was founded in 1935. The museum is operated by four Scottish universities and centres around typical domestic life as lived in this area over several centuries.

Kincraig, about four miles north of Kingussie, is probably best known among visitors for its *Highland Wildlife Park* — a Highland equivalent of the sort of drive-through 'animal kingdoms' that have proved so popular in England, with bison, Soay sheep (as found in the wild only on the remote island of St Kilda), brown bears, wolves, wildcats and many other animals. All of these have at one time lived, or still exist in the north of Scotland. It is not difficult to see — from your car — those animals such as bison and wild horses that roam free within the confines of the park.

At the north end of *Loch Insh*, which lies just east of the village, is *Insh church* — a place of worship for nearly 1300 years.

The important holiday resorts of Aviemore and Carrbridge lie to the north of Kincraig. Aviemore, the best-known of all the Speyside winter-sports centres, has a lot going for it in the summer too. Almost all the activities, the skiing, pony-trekking, fishing, hillwalking, plus indoor amusements like curling, go-karting, bowling, ice-skating, are quite suitable for complete beginners. No one would call the hotels and chalets the most externally beautiful in Scotland, but they are, at best, extremely comfortable and welcoming, and package holidays are available that will suit every pocket. All enquiries should be directed to the *Spey Valley Tourist Organisation*, Aviemore, Highland Region.

Carrbridge, ten miles north of Aviemore along the A9, completes the chain of holiday resorts that will prove of exceptional interest to the visitor who wants to enjoy something of the outdoor life without giving up his creature comforts. Carrbridge is known for *Landmark*, a sophisticated Visitor Centre, with an imaginative exhibition of life and wildlife in the Highlands, a very well stocked bookshop, souvenirs, audio-visual shows, and a nature trail that is modest and suitable for small children.

Dundee to Aberdeen

Travelling eastwards from Dundee, the A930 leads through Broughty Ferry to Carnoustie, one of whose two championship golf courses is said to be the most challenging in the world.

Arbroath Abbey

Further along the coast lies Arbroath, which has long been a seaside resort and shopping centre, with cliff walks and *Cliffs Nature Trail*. Ten miles from the coast here is the *Inchcape* or *Bell Rock*, on a treacherous reef that, over the centuries, has claimed the lives of hundreds of sailors.

Following the A92 northwards for thirteen miles, Montrose is the next town of any size. It is a busy town, with a pleasantly old-fashioned main street, and an air of prosperity that stems from the place's increasing importance in the oil exploration business — for Montrose has an unusual natural and almost landlocked harbour that is much in demand.

From Montrose, a visit via the A935 to the ancient small town of Brechin is recommended. Here, the much restored cathedral makes a fine parish church. Brechin is a good place to break your journey whether you are travelling towards Dundee and Perth or to the north. In the narrow but often busy streets in the centre of the town are some interesting shops, and there are enough ancient buildings to suggest to the visitor much of the character of the place hundreds of years ago.

Well worth the detour from A94 is Edzell, a small town with a wide main street, lying in attractive woody countryside near to the 16th-century tower house of *Edzell Castle*. This is best known for its formal walled garden or 'Pleasance', which is maintained with some similarity to its original form.

Fettercairn is a quiet village through which those visitors who take the very agreeable 'back road', the B974 to Banchory, on the Dee, will pass (see page 61). This lonely road passes through high-lying moorland, then, as it approaches Deeside, becomes wooded and well-protected. It is a delightful way to approach the A93 Aberdeen to Braemar road.

The turretted arch at one end of Fettercairn commemorates a visit by Queen Victoria in 1861. Within a mile of the village lies *Fasque House*, which belongs to the Gladstone family, descendants of the Victorian Prime Minister. This fine mansion with its unique inventory of period contents is now open to the public.

Both the A92 and the A94 are busy roads with heavy commercial traffic, which at certain times of the year is boosted by holiday traffic. The A92 has the advantage of following the coast, and in good weather small coastal villages such as pretty Gourdon and Catterline are tempting. The A94 passes close to the *Howe o' the Mearns* — rich farming country more reminiscent of Herefordshire than Scotland.

Stonehaven is now the headquarters for the recently formed District Council of Kincardine and Deeside. It is a classic small harbour town, with invigorating walks along the protective harbour walls and around the sea-walled Old Town. But the newer side of Stonehaven has produced some interesting small shops and pleasant small cafes. The town has quite a following with people who like seaside holidays away from the crowds. The beach is of shingle and not sand.

Near Stonehaven, *Dunnottar Castle* (via the A92) is well worth a visit. Dunnottar is set dramatically on a rock in the sea a few yards off-shore — but accessible by a path.

The A92 north of Stonehaven follows the coast quite closely, but much of the time one is unaware that the sea is only a mile or two away.

Stonehaven, tranquil, ancient, and well-provided with small hotels and restaurants, is not well-known to visitors. The old town, especially, is worth a detour.

Half a mile from the road at Muchalls, between Aberdeen and Stonehaven, is *Muchalls Castle* — open at limited times to the public. This part of the coast is famous for its great sea-battered rocks, notably *Grim Brigs*: this is more reminiscent of the west coast of Scotland rather than the east. Indeed, the newcomer to Britain probably imagines most of the country around Aberdeen is mountainous. Most Englishmen who don't know Scotland at all certainly do. But it is 'Lowland' in character — until you get sufficiently far west of Aberdeen to be part of *Royal Deeside*, which heralds the approach of mountainous country.

Dunnottar Castle

59

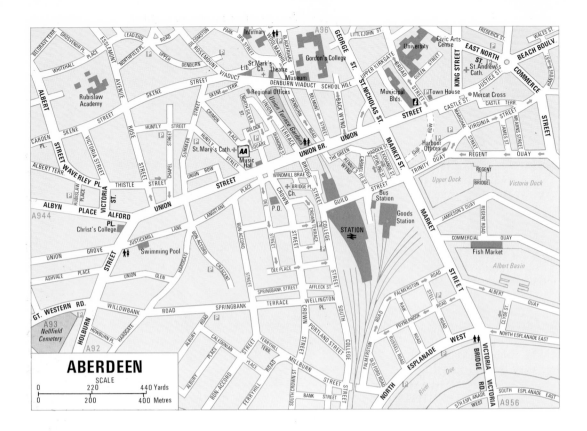

Aberdeen

Aberdeen is one of Scotland's major cities with a population of nearly one quarter of a million. It is a city of character — a medieval university town, European Oil capital, historic burgh, major fishing port and seaside resort.

The first recorded charters of Aberdeen (still preserved in the Town House) were granted by William the Lion in the 12th century. Religious, scholastic and commercial interests have shaped the city through the centuries, and Aberdeen presents vivid contrasts of beach, cliff and harbour, river and woodland, ancient buildings, silver granite and parks. It is Scotland's largest holiday resort, with miles of clean sands, good golf courses and facilities for children.

In addition to its holiday attractions, Aberdeen is, of course, the principal commercial port in the north, and the largest fishery harbour in Scotland. It is also the service centre for North Sea oil rigs. But in spite of the £15 million developments of recent years, most of the harbour remains accessible to the casual visitor. No oil comes ashore at Aberdeen and the nearest rig is miles out at sea, so that the main evidence of the industry is the constant traffic of supply boats.

For those who enjoy the bustle of a busy harbour, the best time for a visit is in the early morning when fish are being auctioned. A quieter view, particularly lovely on summer evenings, is from Greyhope Road on the south of the Dee estuary where inshore fishermen can be watched at work.

With the development of the oil industry Aberdeen has become increasingly cosmopolitan and shops, hotels, pubs and restaurants are many and varied. Standards in the hotels are high, and bed and breakfast accommodation is plentiful.

Amongst the buildings of special interest are *St Machar's Cathedral*, dating from the 14th century; *Kings College* founded in 1494; the famous 14th century *Brig o' Balgownie* with its Cottown of houses dating from the 16th century; *Marischal College*, founded in 1593 as a Protestant rival to Kings College; the 17th century Mercat Cross; *St Nicholas Church*, the 'Mither Kirk' at the centre of the city's life since earliest times; *Provost Ross's House* dating from 1593 and *St Andrews Episcopal Cathedral* commemorating Samuel Seabury, first Bishop of the United States, who was consecrated in Aberdeen in 1748. Art Galleries and museums include *Aberdeen Art Gallery*; *James Dun's House* children's museum; *Provost Skene's House*, one of Aberdeen's oldest dwellings, which has been restored as a museum of domestic and civic life; the *Gordon Highlanders Regimental Museum* and the *Anthropological Museum* in Marischal College. In June each year is the Aberdeen Festival, with a wide variety of events, including Highland Games, and in August the city hosts the International Festival of Youth Orchestras and Performing Arts.

The tourist information office is at St Nicholas House, Broad Street, tel. (0224) 23456, and is open all year round.

Aberdeen is only 1 hour 20 minutes from London by air and has direct air, road and rail links with the other main

Scottish cities, the Western Isles and far north, and the Orkney and Shetland Islands.

Aberdeen to Braemar

and south to Blairgowrie

The A93 road to Banchory, Ballater, Braemar and then southwards towards *Spittal of Glenshee*, Blairgowrie and ultimately, after a distance of about 100 miles, to Perth, is one of the most impressive trunk roads in Scotland — well surfaced, comfortable enough for coaches and cars with trailers, unspoilt for the motorist by the need to negotiate built-up areas (though there are of course speed restrictions through the small towns and villages along the route).

The A93 follows the River Dee as far as Braemar, beyond which that most regal of Scottish rivers departs from the road — except for the more enterprising traveller: there is an easy and worthwhile detour west of Braemar, along the river towards *Mar Lodge*.

Hikers who walk the hills beyond Mar Lodge, west of Braemar, should take care during the stalking season not to disturb the deer which are culled here each autumn to preserve the herds intact and healthy.

Travelling west along the A93 from Aberdeen, there are several places of particular interest, worth stopping for or making short detours to. Just beyond Peterculter lies *Drum Castle* north of the A93. A 13th-century tower house open to the public it is the oldest of the tower houses for which this corner of Scotland is famous.

About five miles west of Drum is another, grander tower house — *Crathes Castle*. This was built about 200 years after Drum, and has superb gardens of nearly 600 acres. The yew trees were planted in 1702. The castle is well known for its elaborate decorated ceilings.

Banchory, just five minutes' drive from Crathes, is the first of several holiday and touring centres that lie along the course of the Dee. There are several hotels and small restaurants, as well as shops and, as a treasured tourist attraction, a salmon leap at the *Bridge of Feugh*. Lavender is grown and distilled near here.

Although traffic is lighter along the A93 west of Banchory the road remains fast and well surfaced. Two miles west of Kincardine O'Neil there are signs for *Craigievar Castle*, another of the tower houses accessible from the A93.

Craigievar, with its recently restored pinkish stonework, its open but commanding position among rolling farms and pleasant moorland, is the outstanding tower house of the region. In the hands of the National Trust for Scotland, whose expert guides convey a sense of how secure and enjoyable life must have been for the families who lived here, the castle has remained essentially as it was built in 1626.

A diversion — north to Speyside

Some drivers may wish to continue north of Craigievar. The A980 connects with roads leading over the Cairngorms towards Grantown-on-Spey. Follow the A980 to just west of

The pinkish stone of Craigievar is like a beacon among the gentle Aberdeenshire hills, drawing visitors to one of the most impressive of all the tower houses.

Alford, then take the A944 westwards as far as the junction with the A97. Then take the A97 going south, for Kildrummy. Just beyond the village the road passes very close to *Kildrummy Castle*, one of the most historic castles in this part of Scotland. It was here that the Jacobite rebellion of 1715 was planned, and after the defeat of the rebels the castle, which had been of great prestige for hundreds of years, fell into disrepair. It is now a ruin, albeit a spectacular one, and is open to the public.

Follow the A97 as far as the junction with the B973, and take the B973 westwards towards Cock Bridge. Just west of Strathdon on this road lies *Corgarff Castle*, which at first sight looks more like an 18th-century mill than what it really is — a 16th century castle with later fortifications. It stood on the all-important military road that led up to the *Moray Firth*. North of Cock Bridge on the A939, Tomintoul is the highest-lying village in the north of Scotland. The buildings in Tomintoul are mainly single-storey, which makes the main street seem higher than it is. The stone buildings are pleasantly uniform.

The highest point of the military road, known as the Lecht road, is between Corgarff and Tomintoul. When the winter snows come, this is always the first road in Scotland to become impassable. Here, at approximately 2000 feet, there are car parking spaces and views of the stupendous primeval moors that stretch towards the highest peaks of the Cairngorms.

As happens so often for carborne travellers in the Highlands, the pleasure of arriving at a sheltered and peaceful valley is enhanced by a sense of relief at leaving behind the wild moors with the often tortuous roads that cross them.

This sensation is particularly strong as one approaches the *Spey Valley*, and Grantown-on-Spey. This solid and prepossessing town was founded, as the name suggests, by the Grant family, whose former home, *Castle Grant*, is now deserted. Grantown's wide and tree-lined main street is a pleasant introduction to the string of small towns and often lively villages that characterise the valley. This part of Scotland is now one of the outstanding winter sports venues in Europe.

But it is not exclusively used in winter. Many a city-dweller living in Edinburgh, Manchester and London comes here to escape for a few hours or days into the *Cairngorms* and the *Monadhliath Mountains ('Grey' Mountains)* for deerstalking, fishing, grouse-shooting, or just hill-walking. Despite tourist activity in this part of the Highlands, both mountain ranges are still comparatively neglected. What roads there are, apart from the main roads, tend to peter out very quickly, and even if you are travelling by Range Rover, it soon becomes advisable to go by foot.

The junction of the A95 from Grantown with the A9 is more or less mid-way between two small but celebrated resorts, Aviemore and Carrbridge.

Back on the A93, Aboyne is an exceptionally large and attractive village. The huge green to the south of the main road is the setting for the *Aboyne Games* which are held every autumn.

Accessible from Aboyne is the B976, which comes close to the southern bank of the Dee near Kincardine O'Neil, and this road follows the river's course closely upstream to just east of Balmoral. Tree-lined, with frequent pretty views of the river, the B976 is a winding, slower but practical alternative to the busier A93.

Ballater lost much of its former glory when the railway station that used to serve the royal castle of *Balmoral* just ten miles west of the town, was closed. The railway line would have run even closer to this favourite royal home if Queen Victoria had not opposed it so violently. She was in favour of railways, but not if they were likely to disturb her peace and quiet.

The station buildings remain in use as a Tourist Information Centre and Council offices, and this small town has a prosperous, comfortable air with its shops and small hotels, nestling among the foothills of the Cairngorms.

To the south of Ballater an unclassified road along *Glen Muick* leads to *Loch Muick*, a distance of approximately thirteen miles. From Loch Muick, which is exceptionally deep, there is a possible approach to the famous peak of *Lochnagar* (3786 feet) that dominates the skyline between Ballater and Braemar. Though even its peak is accessible to the strong and well-equipped hillwalker, some of Lochnagar's wildest and rockiest corries have never been climbed, and this impressive mountain has been the inspiration of poets and writers — not least of them Byron:

'Over the crags that are wild and majestic / the steep frowning glories of dark Lochnagar.' Just east of Balmoral, whose grounds are open to the public at certain times of the year, lies *Crathie Church*, whose services are sometimes attended by the royal family when they are in residence during the late summer and early autumn. In the churchyard there is a memorial to *John Brown*, Queen Victoria's favourite servant.

Balmoral can easily be missed by visitors approaching from the east, because it stands back from the A93 on the left hand side and presents a bolder front to people coming from the direction of Braemar. When the Queen stays at Balmoral her visit usually coincides with the world-famous *Braemar Gathering*, probably the best known of all the traditional highland games. The event, held in early September, attracts crowds of over 20,000. Accommodation in hotels and guesthouses over a huge radius should be reserved well in advance. The appearance of the royal family and 'tossing the caber' are the high points of this one day event, which is held at the Princess Royal Park.

Braemar Castle

Braemar Castle stands to the east of the town. Built by the Earl of Mar in 1628, it has had a dramatic history, especially during the Jacobite uprisings of 1715 and 1745 when the castle assumed a strategic importance on the military road from Perth to the coast north of Grantown. As you approach Braemar from the east, the comfortable, rambling and hospitable *Invercauld Arms* lies on the left. The hotel was built on the site on which the Jacobite banner was raised in September, 1715. And it was from *Invercauld House* (visible from the road as one approaches Braemar, to the north, but not open to the public) that the Earl of Mar called out the clans in support of the *Old Pretender*. Except when its population swells twentyfold, at the time of the Gathering, Braemar seems smaller than most people imagine it will be. It lies on the edge of wild moors and hills where stags are hunted and huge salmon caught, in surroundings that are remarkable even in a land of scenic superlatives.

Crathes, at the eastern end of Deeside, is just one of a magnificent array of castles, or 'tower houses', in this part of the country. Crathes itself is surrounded by superb gardens.

A beautiful, wide stretch of the river Dee extends west of Braemar, while the main road bends southwards towards *Glen Clunie* and the increasingly important skiing and pony trekking centre at Spittal of Glenshee.

The A93 climbs to almost 2500 feet at the Cairnwell ski centre chairlift; in under ten miles the character of the road changes from easy and meandering to steep and narrow, but since road improvements, the driver no longer has to negotiate uncomfortable bends at the *Devil's Elbow*. The Spittal of Glenshee takes its name from a hospital, or hostel for travellers, which existed here during the 14th and 15th centuries. The road then runs through lonely *Glenshee* towards Blairgowrie. As the A93 rose into the hills south of Braemar, so it descends to Blairgowrie, on the edge of the foothills of the Cairngorms and, effectively, the southern boundary of the Highlands.

From Blairgowrie the A923, westwards, reaches Dunkeld, seven miles away. The road is interesting for the small lochs one passes on the left hand side of the road, one of which, *Loch Clunie*, has an island that bears the remains of the *Castle of Clunie*, built almost 500 years ago. And the road promises exciting things to come, because in the distance, about twenty miles away as the crow flies, are the peaks west of Loch Tay that include *Ben Lawers* — almost 4000 feet high.

The A93, as it continues southwards from Blairgowrie towards Perth (approximately thirteen miles) passes close to the village of Meikleour, and the nearby *Meikleour House*, home of the Marquess of Lansdowne. The house is well known for its great *Beech Hedge* which was planted in 1746, the year after Bonnie Prince Charlie's abortive attempt to gain the throne. The hedge runs alongside the main road for about a quarter of a mile.

Scone Palace (pronounced Skoon), previously one of the most important houses in Scotland, lies two miles north of Perth, just south of the racecourse (National Hunt rules only, not flat racing).

Part of the original 16th-century house, where all Scottish kings until James I were crowned (as was Charles II in 1661) has been incorporated in the present mansion, which was completed in 1808. The *Stone of Scone*, or Stone of Destiny, was brought here in about 830. Believed to have a mystic quality, and undoubtedly possessed of symbolic importance for Scots for many hundreds of years, it is now incorporated in the Coronation Chair in Westminster Abbey in London.

Aberdeen to Inverness

The main road from Aberdeen to Inverness is the A96, via the attractive, partly-Georgian towns of Inverurie, Huntly and Fochabers. The coastal road to Peterhead, Fraserburgh and Banff takes us to a corner of Scotland that few tourists see.

Close to the small town of Oldmeldrum, off the B999, lies Tolquhon Castle, a picturesque ruin at first sight, but actually a lived-in and sophisticated 16th-century house. The nearby Pitmedden Gardens are a bonus if you come this way.

Peterhead is reminiscent of a small Aberdeen: it has the same greyish-pink granite buildings and it has survived the

Tolquhon Castle

vagaries — or, one should say, the demise — of herring fishing, before being projected well and truly into the late 20th century with the arrival of the 'oil men'.

Fraserburgh, an industrial as well as a fishing town, has a harbour, beach, lighthouse (formerly a tower), and a burial mound at Memsie.

Peterhead harbour

Back on the coast, Banff, Portsoy and Cullen all have small harbours used nowadays mainly for leisure and small-scale fishing. These unassuming, often windswept places are most interesting. Banff is a small shopping centre with many ancient and interesting buildings. The town has seven comfortable hotels, which makes it a worthwhile stopping place. The most famous building of all is *Duff House*, which has a bizarre story attached to it. The Earl of Fife, who had the house built (it was modelled on the *Villa Borghese*, in Rome) quarrelled with the architect and never lived in the house, even though the greater part of it was completed. The house is now open to the public from April to September.

Fochabers is the headquarters of the massive food producers, Baxters, whose tinned soups and other canned Scottish delicacies reach the farthest corners of the globe. The country between Fochabers, Elgin, Forres and Nairn is comparatively flat, but there are many points of interest.

From Forres, for example, the B9011 runs north to Findhorn, renowned for its *commune*; *Findhorn Bay* is extremely well sheltered and marvellous for sailing.

Cawdor Castle, where Macbeth is said to have murdered Duncan, has a 15th-century tower surrounded by 16th-century buildings. Much restoration work has been done, and the gardens are delightful.

Nairn is an attractive seaside town, with good facilities. South of Nairn, *Cawdor Castle* at Cawdor on the B9090 has been extremely well restored. This castle, made famous by its Shakespearean connections (Macbeth, Thane of Cawdor), is open to the public, as are its beautiful gardens.

Note: *Culloden Moor* and Inverness are included in the North chapter.

Hotel and Guest House Accommodation

DARROCH LEARG HOTEL
BALLATER—ON ROYAL DEESIDE, GRAMPIAN

"A Lovely Hotel in a Delightful Setting"

In 4 acres of garden and woodland overlooking the golf course and the River Dee, commanding glorious views of hills and mountains.

25 Bedrooms—10 with private bathrooms

Send for illustrated colour brochure to:

Resident Proprietors:
Mr and Mrs C. D. FRANKS
or Telephone Ballater (03382) 443

AA*   ABERDEENSHIRE   RAC*
THE LODGE HOTEL
OLD RAYNE

Central for touring the North-East. Six bedrooms most with private bathroom. Centrally heated throughout. Real Ale. Friendly service. Brochure and tariff on request.

Old Rayne, Insch, Aberdeenshire AB5 6RY. Tel. Old Rayne (04645) 205.

"ASHLEA" ARDERSIER, Inverness-shire. Bed & Breakfast. Very comfortable. From £3.50. Double & single rooms. Mrs J. Smart. Tel. Ard 2212.

NAIRN
ARDGOUR HOTEL
SEAFIELD STREET

Unlicensed small family hotel. Colour TV Lounge. Bed and Breakfast £4.00 (£5.00 June to Sept. incl.) Optional 3 course dinner with tea/coffee £2.00. Tea/biscuits 9.30 p.m. included. Reductions for children sharing.

Phone Nairn (0667) 54230
Mrs Jane Hutchison

ROTTAL LODGE
GLEN CLOVA, ANGUS

Beautifully situated in the heart of the glen, we proudly offer real Highland hospitality. Good food, based on locally grown produce, carefully chosen wines.

A fine centre for fishing, golf and exploring the many beautiful glens and surrounding countryside.

Brochure on request.

Telephone 057 55 224 and 242

ROYAL HOTEL
FORTROSE, BLACK ISLE
Comfortable family hotel. Golf course, sailing, interesting walks. Ideal for touring Highlands. Good Scottish food.

PITTODRIE HOUSE HOTEL
Pitcaple 202.
Country House Hotel.

BETTYHILL HOTEL
BETTYHILL   SUTHERLAND

The ideal choice for a fishing holiday or a restful break. First class cuisine. Fully licensed. Salmon and Brown Trout Fishing. A Botanist's Paradise. Open all year.

Telephone Bettyhill (0641-2) 352

THE BOAT HOTEL

SPEYSIDE'S POPULAR SPORTING HOLIDAY HOTEL
Resident Proprietors:
Mr and Mrs D. B. Wilson
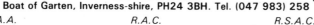

Boat of Garten, Inverness-shire, PH24 3BH. Tel. (047 983) 258

A.A.   R.A.C.   R.S.A.C.

Come and enjoy a splendid holiday at The Boat Hotel. With its country house atmosphere and excellent food, the Boat is the ideal hotel to enjoy a Scottish sporting holiday at its best. A FINE 18-HOLE GOLF COURSE and TENNIS COURTS, RIGHT BESIDE THE HOTEL. Golf School weeks with professional tuition 30 April-7 May, 24 Sept.-1 Oct, 1 Oct.-8 Oct.

Fishing on the famous River Spey—permits from hotel

Another four golf courses within 30 minutes car drive from the hotel. Within 15 minutes drive: walking, climbing, SKI-ING, indoor swimming pool, skating, cinema. The situation of the Boat makes it perfect as a motoring centre.

Skye and
the Western Isles

The importance of Western Scotland's roll-on, roll-off ferries is clear when one realises that it is possible to take one's car right round the Outer Hebrides archipelago — or as it is more generally known, the Western Isles — even on a trip of a few days' duration. It is important, though, to read the ferry timetables and, at busy periods, to book ahead. The same applies to accommodation.

Bridges or causeways now link the smaller islands, and these help us to make the strung-out islands of Barra, South Uist, Benbecula, North Uist, Harris and Lewis into virtually one island — the 'Long Island', as it is often called.

While it is officially within the Highland Region, Skye has much of the Hebridean character, even though it is so easily and quickly accessible from the mainland. The five-minute crossing from Kyle of Lochalsh to Kyleakin is more than just another routine trip. It is an adventure into a romantic island in the Atlantic. The true source of the name 'Skye' is not known, but one explanation is that it comes from *sgiath*, the Gaelic for 'wing'.

Skye has the most exciting peaks in the whole of Western Scotland — even for experienced climbers. And it has a romantic past, rich in legend, that makes it somehow familiar even to people who have never set foot in the Hebrides.

Lewis and Harris are really one island. Not only are they easily the biggest of the Hebridean islands, but they form the third largest land mass in the whole of the British Isles. Despite being one island, Harris and Lewis are very different in character — Harris is as rocky and mountainous as Lewis is low-lying and predominantly covered with bleak and windy peat moors. Lewis is famous for its fishing, and *Harris Tweed* — the cottage industries that produce Harris Tweed are actually more common on Lewis than on Harris, although tweed is produced on both. Gaelic is spoken widely on Lewis — more so than on Skye — and there is even a small, but well integrated, Gaelic-speaking Pakistani community. Harris is better known for its rare birds — eagles and falcons as well as sea birds — and its deer forests and grouse shooting. North Harris is more mountainous than South Harris, whose western coast has some fine beaches and green headlands.

Some of the most beautiful and least crowded sandy beaches in the whole of Britain lie on the Atlantic (western) side of the 'Long Isle'. The interior is normally boggy and peaty and, generally, hills and mountains lie on the eastern side. Accommodation is not plentiful, though frequently of a surprisingly high standard. Bed-and-breakfast accommodation is often extremely good.

Much of one's enjoyment of the Western Isles can depend on the vicissitudes of the weather, for prolonged rain or even drizzle can be totally demoralising. In good spring or autumn weather, a prolonged visit to North Uist, Benbecula, South Uist and Barra can make one feel that these are, indeed, the 'Enchanted Isles'.

Ferry passengers making the short crossing from Kyle of Lochalsh to Kyleakin, on Skye, cannot miss Castle Moil – once a lookout against marauding Vikings.

Skye

Of all the Scottish islands Skye has the firmest hold on people's imagination. It has inspired some famous folk songs, its history has elements of the tragedy and romance that colours the Highlands and Islands, and its sea-wracked coastline, mountains, and great variety of scenery make it an outstanding holiday venue. Even though Skye is a very popular place to visit, there is always somewhere quiet to explore, even on a warm Bank Holiday.

There are three ferry crossings; one from Kyle of Lochalsh, on the mainland, to Kyleakin, takes less than five minutes. The trip from Mallaig to Armdale, is more of an adventure for first-time visitors, taking approximately 45 minutes. This ferry can be more convenient for those travelling from the south, but it is, of course, a good deal costlier. The third

crossing, another short one, is from the picturesque Glenelg to Kylerhea.

The quality of the roads on Skye varies. Although improvements are always being made, progress will not be as fast as on some comparatively remote roads on the mainland. Skye is not a place to visit if you are in a hurry. Most visitors will start their tour of the island at Kyleakin, but if they do it is well worth turning off before Broadford on the A851 to Ardvasar, to see *Armadale Castle*. This early 19th-century gothic building is the seat of the Macdonalds of Sleat, who, with the MacLeods of Dunvegan, are hereditary chiefs of the island. The castle gardens are open to the public.

North of the castle an unclassified road towards the west coast of this southerly foot of Skye has good views of the small Hebridean island of Rhum, and takes one through lonely moorland country before it doubles back to the A851 Broadford road.

In summer Broadford is a busy little town. Lying on Broadford Bay, it has well stocked shops, hotels and bars. It is a useful provisioning place for the many campers and caravanners who visit the island.

Just north of Broadford, to the right of the road, lies the island of Scalpay. Oysters are found near here, and this was formerly an assembly point for massive herring fleets. But visitors are more likely to visit Raasay, just to the north. There are ferries from Sconser, hired privately, and the boats plying between Kyle of Lochalsh and Portree call at the island. Samuel Johnson and James Boswell wrote vividly of their visit to Raasay in the journal based on their Hebridean tour. They were royally entertained at *Raasay House* (still standing) in 1773. Of the island Boswell wrote 'Such a seat of hospitality amidst the winds and waters fills the imagination with a delightful contrariety of images. Without, the rough ocean and the rocky land, the beating billows and the howling storm; within is plenty, elegance, beauty and gaiety, the song and the dance'.

Also of interest is *Brochel Castle*, worth the journey to the end of the only road on the island.

Portree, nine miles north of the A850 junction with the A863 Dunvegan road, is the only town of any size on Skye. The name means *'port of the King'*, and was adopted by what was then the small village of Kiltaragleann after a visit by James V. Portree is vital for communication and supplies from the mainland, and it is a busy administrative centre for most of the affairs of the island. There are shops and several good hotels; one outstanding hotel in the area is the *Skeabost Bridge Hotel*, five miles north of Portree on the Dunvegan road. The setting is superb, the food is good, and the welcome is warm — literally, because there are log fires in even cool or drizzly weather.

Portree lies at the southern end of the Trotternish peninsula, another of the easily identifiable great pro-

Highland cattle on Skye. The island is accessible and geared to tourists, but its bleak and beautiful wastes can provide solitude for many visitors.

truberances of this weirdly shaped island. With the exception of Minginish where the Cuillins are, this is scenically the most impressive part of Skye.

The main road from Portree to Uig, from where car ferries make the two hour trip to Harris and North Uist, is the A856; beyond here the road continues as the A855, completing the circular tour of the peninsula. Along this road lie *Kilmuir*, burial site of Flora MacLeod, who died in 1790, and *Duntulm Castle*, the ancient seat of the Macdonalds of the Isles in the north of Skye. Further round, the road runs very close to the dramatic peak of *The Storr* (2358 feet), near whose foot stands the famous black obelisk, *The Old Man of Storr* (160 feet).

The road to Dunvegan is narrow and of variable quality; the countryside is mainly open moorland. Before the descent to Dunvegan, the B886 runs part of the way up into the Vaternish peninsula. Near the end of this road is the village of Stein, where, at the end of the 18th century, attempts were made to offset the disastrous effects of emigration — mainly to North America — by setting up a fishing industry.

Dunvegan Castle

Dunvegan is a place of pilgrimage for MacLeods all over the world, for *Dunvegan Castle* has been the seat of the clan chiefs for hundreds of years. The situation of the castle is very dramatic, rising sheer from the almost perpendicular rock, but bordered on the eastern side by gardens and woods. It has dungeons, trap doors, a Fairy Tower, a portcullis on the seaward side — in short, all one can expect from a castle.

Until 1976 the clan chief was Dame Flora MacLeod of MacLeod, daughter of Sir Reginald MacLeod, the 27th chief. She died in her mid-nineties after tirelessly devoting the equivalent of most people's lifetime to the castle and the prestige of the MacLeod clan all over the world.

The south coast of Duirinish has some of the most impressive cliff scenery in Scotland. The unclassified road to *Orbost House*, overlooking Loch Bracadale, brings motorists as close as they will get to the famous basalt stacks known as *MacLeod's Maidens*, just off the southernmost tip of Duirnish: legend says that these two landmarks are the haunt of mermaids.

The A863 south of Duirnish (which is more nearly an island than most of Skye's great promontories) runs towards Loch Harport, where, at Carbost, is the distillery for the world-famous Talisker whisky, the only malt whisky distilled on Skye, but one of the best of all malts. South of Loch Harport and Glen Drynoch lie the Cuillins. Though these dramatic peaks are associated in most people's minds with Skye as readily as is Bonnie Prince Charlie, those who stick to the main roads miss the chance of even a close sight of this wild country. You do not have to be a climber — even energetic walkers can see some of the most dramatic parts of the Cuillins, by walking up *Glen Sligachan* for example. And drivers can take the unclassified road off the B8809 Drynoch/Carbost road towards Loch Brittle, on the southern side of the island. There is a sandy bay here, a good camping site and, at Glenbrittle itself, a base for climbing some of the highest peaks of the Cuillins. The highest peak of all, *Sgùrr Alasdair* (3309 feet) is named after Alexander Nicolson, who climbed the mountain in 1873.

Strenuous efforts are being made to revive Gaelic on Skye as a widely spoken language, and to prevent it from becoming something quaint that only appears in folk songs and whimsical books of poetry. The signs are that the rescue attempt will be successful, gathering strength as it does from the more westerly islands where Gaelic is widely used. The holidaymaker will hear songs and talks in Gaelic on his hotel radio and in pubs and shops, and the air of mystique it conveys adds interest to this most easterly of the Western Isles.

Barra

Barra's airport, though not the most visited, is probably the best known in the Hebrides, for the planes land on a sandy beach washed twice daily by the tide. This island was the setting for Compton Mackenzie's novel *Whisky Galore* (Barra being one of several islands on which that itinerant novelist lived during his long life). His story was based on the foundering of the 1200-ton vessel 'Politician' in February 1941. She was carrying 20,000 cases of whisky, bound for New York. The occasional bottle from that cargo is still produced, but none are drinkable, being full of oil and grime.

In Castlebay, the principal village on the island, lies *Kisimul Castle*, home of the Macneils of Barra (whose laird, an American lawyer, is resident in New York for most of the

Barra airport

From Kilbride, on South Uist, looking south to Barra. In calm and summery conditions the Western Isles, with their perfect sandy beaches and their blue waters, can rival the Aegean.

year). It is an exceptionally well restored castle, rich in history and legend.

There is one circular road on Barra, almost as memorable for its designation (A888) as its pleasant 14-mile course.

There is a string of smaller islands south of Barra, only one of which, Vatersay, is inhabited. There are also boat trips in summer to Mingulay, famous for the colonies of seabirds (particularly fulmars and kittiwakes) that nest on its 820-foot cliffs.

The trip to Mingulay from Barra takes about two hours. In good weather the place is beautiful, with all the remote grandeur of St Kilda, far out in the Atlantic.

A trip to Barra alone may seem expensive and time-consuming, but the car ferry which comes from Oban four times a week also calls at Lochboisdale, on South Uist, and from there is a road from Lochmaddy, on North Uist. Lochmaddy is a ferry link for Uig on Skye, and Tarbert, on Harris. Since bridges and causeway roads were built, these Western Isles have seemed less like separate islands than part of one whole. They all have fine beaches, a peaty and boggy interior, and lochs and mountains on the east side — and in the right conditions can seem a demi-paradise.

South Uist, North Uist, Benbecula

Lochboisdale is the main centre of population on South Uist. There are hotels here much favoured by anglers, who find among the west coast lochs some of the best fishing in the whole of Scotland. The birdlife is remarkable: there are a number of sanctuaries and observation points, and, in addition to the colonies of seabirds, these islands offer some rare marshland birds, greylag geese, mute swans and wild-fowl and waders. There is good hill-climbing, too, on and around *Beinn Mhor* (2034 feet).

Before the construction of the causeway road from South Uist to Benbecula and from Benbecula to North Uist the fords were dangerous, but there are no such problems now. Creagorry, on Benbecula, has some accommodation, and this is the best point from which to explore this mainly flat island with its abiding memories of the defeated Young Pretender after his escape from the mainland in 1746.

North Uist looks from the air like an elaborate piece of green lace. It is so studded with lochs and lochans, and so riddled on its northern coast with bays and sea-lochs that it forms an other-worldly landscape and a paradise on earth for anglers and ornithologists.

Lochmaddy, with a population of 400, is hardly a town but, on account of its hospital, its tourist bureau, its shops and its bank, it is more than a village. One of North Uist's claims to fame is that this was the first place in the Hebrides where potatoes were planted (1743). Seaweed was harvested here for half a century for the kelp that it produced, and at one point the North Uist population was over 5000. The industry is still an important one in the island.

St Kilda

The tiny minority of travellers who make the 95-mile trip from Oban to the Atlantic island of St Kilda, 45 miles or so from Benbecula normally call at Lochmaddy on their way to and from this now deserted and lonely archipelago (St Kilda comprises seven islands, Hirta being the only one which has ever supported human life). Until the 1930s St Kilda maintained an independent and functioning society. The National Trust for Scotland, which owns and administers St Kilda, arranges working-party and 'safari' trips; the latter demands less involvement in cooking, cleaning, etc. The tours last approximately two weeks and cost from about £130 per person for the basic 'holiday'. For energetic people in good health this is a rare chance to spend some time on a beautiful, if barren, distant island with a fascinating past. Now it is the huge colonies of sea-birds, including fulmars, petrels and gannets who really possess the island. Until the St Kildans became tourist conscious, and developed a more sophisticated economy, they lived mainly on these birds.

The Sound of Taransay, off the west coast of Harris. The vast stretches of clean and golden sand are perhaps the most underused beaches in the world.

Lewis and Harris

Lewis and Harris make up one island, the largest in the Western Isles. It is nearly 500 square miles — bigger than Skye. There are very few trees, and the land is mainly composed of peat bog.

There are marked differences between Harris and Lewis. Harris has more high hills and rocks — one summit, *Clisham*, is 2622 feet high, and represents a challenge for even experienced rock climbers. Apart from Sgùrr Alasdair on Skye, it is the highest peak in the whole of the Hebrides. Much of Harris is a 'deer forest' — in most places a treeless one. It attracts fishermen and hunters: there are red deer, grouse, mountain hare, geese and pigeons, salmon and sea trout.

Tarbert, the port of entry for Harris, is nearly equidistant from Lochmaddy, on North Uist, and Uig on Skye, and both places are served by the same car ferry. The run in either direction takes about two hours.

The name Tarbert, as we have seen elsewhere, denotes a narrow neck of land. The town — again, a courtesy title! — lies sheltered among bare, rocky hills. There is accommodation, mainly bed-and-breakfast, and even this can be snapped up quickly in the summer months, and prior booking is essential. But this is something that applies generally to the Western Isles.

An exciting road to travel is the unclassified one to Rodel, near the southernmost tip of Harris. At Rodel, *St Clement's Church* (early 16th century) is worth visiting. Return by the A859, which runs as close to the west coast as the former runs to the east coast. Progress is slow, and at least two hours

Island-scape on South Harris. Though Lewis and Harris form one landmass, the former is generally flat, the latter more mountainous.

should be allowed for the round trip. A couple of miles northwest of Rodel on the A859 is Leverburgh where attempts to create a fishing industry were made by Lord Leverhulme. There is a passenger ferry from Leverburgh to Newton Ferry, on North Uist. This calls on most days at Berneray — an island with about 200 inhabitants. From *Chaipaval* (1092 feet) on Toe Head — an easy climb — there are superb views in clear weather of North Uist.

The main road, the A859, runs east of the Clisham, but the B887 to Hushinish is more interesting. It passes close to the ruins of a former whaling station near the village and, about four miles south of the village is *Amhuinnsuidhe Castle*, built in 1868 (pronounced Amin-suey: not open to the public). It was here that James Bridie wrote *Mary Read*. Hushinish is a beautiful place, with sandy beaches and sheltered inlets.

Stornoway is the biggest town on the Harris/Lewis landmass, and lies at the end of an often turbulent ferry crossing from Ullapool. It is the administrative capital of the Western Isles, and, hotel accommodation is generally of a high standard — there are two three-star hotels and one two-star hotel, plus several smaller hotels and guest-houses. (As a rule, hotel accommodation in the Highlands and Islands is of a slightly higher standard — star for star — than elsewhere in Scotland. This is partly because remote hotels become a focus for local activity and because they deal less with casual passing trade than with holidaymakers and sportsmen who base themselves in a particular hotel for several days at a time.)

Stornoway has an airport with connections from Glasgow. It is an important fishing port, despite the decline of the herring industry, and a welcoming and prosperous community. The name of the town comes from the Norse, and means 'anchor bay'. A glance at the map will show why it was chosen as an anchorage.

Many visitors will be surprised by how flat the country around Stornoway is, and the town has spread comfortably into the hinterland so that it looks even bigger, in terms of population, than it actually is. They will be surprised too by the unexpected sight of *Lews Castle*, a massive Victorian gothic fantasy built in the 1860s and presented to the town by the island's great benefactor, Lord Leverhulme. There is a golf course in the grounds, and walks, open to the public, through the rhododendron gardens.

North and west of Stornoway, via the A857 through barren moorland, are several points of interest. The *Butt of Lewis* is the northernmost point of the island; from here, in the right conditions, can be seen the high peaks of Sutherland, on the mainland, about 40 miles away to the east.

From nearby *Port of Ness*, gannet hunters still sail once a year to the remote island of *Sula Sgeir*, about 30 miles away, to

The standing stones, Callanish

A black house

live in stone bothies and collect 'gugas', or young gannets — considered a great delicacy locally.

Callanish, on the A858 (the almost circular road that runs from Stornoway to Varvas), is famed for the *Callanish Standing Stones*, reminiscent of Stonehenge, in Wiltshire, but not so ancient. The stones are believed to have astrological and astronomical significance, and to be about 3500 years old.

At Carloway, on the A858, about five miles north of Callanish, is a well-preserved Pictish *broch*, or round tower. Its ruins are up to thirty feet high. It is reckoned that such buildings were used as look-out towers and forts during the Iron Age. At Bragar are the remains of a building of similar function, *Dun Loch an Duna*, and at Ballantrushal is an eighteen-foot high monolith known as the *Thrushell Stone*.

Also worth seeing on Lewis are the *folk museum* at Shawbost, between Carloway and Barvas; and between Shawbost and Barvas, the restored *black house* at Arnol. It was not bad planning that created the Harris/Lewis 'black houses', sooty and without proper chimneys, for soot made good manure, something which was sadly lacking on these barren western outposts. Until the mid-19th century, cattle and people shared these long houses, and even used the same entrance. Although there was sometimes a skylight, this soon became obscured by soot, and the entrance was the main source of light. Once a year, especially in the spring, the accumulated cow-dung was removed from the floor of the house. These houses, too, were designed to withstand the all-too-frequent gales that blow up across the Atlantic.

Tweed mills producing Harris tweed are open at certain times to the public, and woollen goods of very superior quality may usually be bought at advantageous prices.

In most parts of Lewis, on the coast, there is good safe bathing, fishing for salmon and trout, and golf. And if the flat countryside of Lewis begins to pall, then the hills of Harris are not far away.

Harris tweed

Harris tweed is also produced on other islands of the Outer Hebrides, and to claim the name it must be hand-woven. It is produced in cottages and on crofts. Until recent years time-honoured local vegetable dyes were used to colour the cloth, but a wider range of colours is now available. There are over 5000 patterns. In such a labour-intensive industry, expenses are high — and the cost of the cloth is aggravated by the high freight charges involved in getting the finished product to its retail outlets. Harris tweed is exported all over the world.

The North

The journey to Inverness or to Skye from south of the Border is enough of an adventure for most people for them never to consider travelling further north. Yet the far north of Scotland is not just an extension of the much more popular Central Highlands (and the north west is both more exciting and more accessible than a casual glance at the map would indicate).

It is a drive of only 1½ hours or thereabouts from Inverness to Ullapool, through some dramatic and geologically very old countryside (the imposing 2399-foot peak of *Suilven*, which lies to the north, rests on rock that is 2700 million years old), and at every other twist and turn of the lonely roads are scenes that have remained more or less unchanged for centuries.

Far more people reach the renowned land's end of the north east of Scotland, John o'Groats, than ever see Cape Wrath and, pleasant though the towns of Wick and Thurso are, the low-lying and fertile county of Caithness cannot match in drama the breathtaking scenery of parts of Sutherland. But readers who have left the north west out of their plans this time, can take comfort from the fact that there can always be a next time. Little is going to change.

For a century or more, ever since the Victorians discovered that, courtesy of the London and North Eastern Railway, overnight sleepers could whisk them into the Highlands to some draughty hunting lodge, this part of Scotland has been the preserve of sportsmen. But you do not have to have a gun or a rod to enjoy yourself here, just a fondness for being the only person or group for a dozen square miles, or for wandering alone along a wide, sandy beach on an August Bank Holiday.

Inverness has been included in this section because most travellers who make it to the far north will go through it. And it is quite a tradition for those making for Sutherland via Motorail or hire car to take breakfast at the Station Hotel after alighting from the overnight sleeper. Without attempting to elevate the pleasures of rail travel over those of car travel we look at how it is possible to continue by rail as far as Thurso and Wick, one of the most exhilarating trips in Europe. We look at the Black Isle (really a peninsula), the northernmost stretches of the A9 along the north east coast of the mainland, and the tortuous, narrower roads along the west and the north coasts.

From certain points on the mainland the Western Isles can be seen 25 or 30 miles away to the west; and from John o'Groats and Dunnet Head there are clear views of the Orkney Islands. From Scrabster, just north of Thurso, runs the key ferry service to Orkney; and another runs from Ullapool to Stornoway — so that even these apparently remote towns play a vital role in this northern communication network.

Inverness

Inverness is the administrative headquarters for the huge new Highland region and has for a long time been the most important town in the Highlands. The town has no great claims to beauty, but it is a worthwhile place to stop during any 'grand tour' of the north. There are several good hotels, the most famous of which is probably the *Station Hotel* — some of whose rooms actually overlook the station platforms. Many thousands of travellers alighting from the overnight sleeper here have enjoyed a substantial traditional breakfast before starting out for points north and west.

There is an airport six miles to the north east, close to the south shore of the *Moray Firth*. Access by air is thus as practicable as access by train for travellers who prefer to pick up a hire car than to drive their own car as far north as this. There are several hire car firms in the town.

Inverness is an important shopping centre, and for those visitors who stay more than a couple of hours, there are points of interest in the *Castle* (19th-century, used now as local government offices and law courts) and the *Cathedral* (also 19th-century, with a richly decorated interior). The new *Eden Court Theatre* is an excellent focus of entertainment, and the *Museum*, several of whose exhibits commemorate Inverness's strategic importance during the Jacobite rebellions is worth a visit. The *Battle of Culloden* was fought just four miles from here, on what is now known as *Culloden Moor*. On the Castle esplanade there is a statue to *Flora Macdonald*, who helped Bonnie Prince Charlie to escape after his crushing defeat at the battle, which took place on 16 April 1746, at the very end of his campaign.

Culloden is well commemorated by the *Visitor Centre* on the site of the battle, and by a memorial stone. There is a museum in a stone-and-thatched cottage that was *in situ* at the time of the battle — a strange juxtaposition of domesticity and horror. Charles's 5000 hungry troops were half-exhausted by an all-night march before they even took on the Duke of Cumberland's forces in this last desperate bid by the Jacobites for the throne. A quarter of Charles's men were killed in the space of 55 minutes. The rest managed to escape. Culloden was the last battle to be fought on Scottish soil.

In order to prevent any recurrence of the Highlanders' revolt against the Crown, a series of repressive measures was devised and *Fort George*, to the north of Inverness, was reinforced. The Fort stands at the meeting point of military roads along which troops could be quickly marched. It had been built well before the Jacobite uprisings, but it enjoyed a second lease of life during the latter part of the 18th century.

Kessock Ferry, just north of the centre of Inverness via the B9161, is the most direct means of access to the *Black Isle* — really a peninsula, fairly low lying and known for its fertile farmland. The name probably comes from a mistranslation of *St Duthac* into the Gaelic *dubh* which means 'black'. St Duthac was born at Tain, on the *Dornoch Firth*, in about AD 1000. A bridge is to be built at Kessock, and also, possibly, at Invergordon, across the *Cromarty Firth*. Though this will make access to the Black Isle much easier, and benefit local farming and industry, it will inevitably detract from the present pleasing 'island' atmosphere.

Inverness to the North West

Inverness represents the northernmost point of most people's

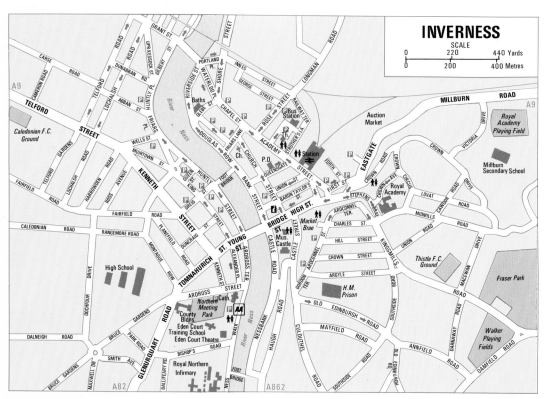

Mellon Udrigle. This curiously-named place on Gruinard Bay enjoys the beauty and serenity so typical of Scotland's north west.

sightseeing ambitions in Scotland, but the 1½ hour hop from Inverness to Ullapool brings the lonely beauty of the far north west closer than many visitors would imagine.

The scenery on the Inverness to Ullapool route changes dramatically from mile to mile, but the road is fast and easy. The route begins via the A9, along the *Beauly Firth*, and runs for part of the distance alongside the railway. Beauly itself — the name probably comes from the French 'beau lieu' — is a village which straggles along either side of a wide street. There are some well-stocked and welcoming shops — including one selling tweeds, knitwear and a big range of traditional, 'sensible' clothes. More like something from the 1930s than the 1970s, it is pleasant to browse in.

The route leaves the A9 at Muir of Ord, gateway to the Black Isle, and diverges north west along the A832 towards Garve. Nearby Strathpeffer, a clearly signed and easy detour, is a former spa town that stands below the great mass of *Ben Wyvis* (3433 feet). The town has several hotels and, in its wooded setting and with its golf courses, tennis courts and shops — plus the 'optional extras' of the still-functioning pump room — is an inviting prospect.

As the A832 approaches Garve it rejoins the railway. It is by now the famous *West Highland Line*, which links Inverness and Kyle of Lochalsh. It is a three-hour run, with two or three trains a day and occasionally the bonus of an observation coach. The line is not only a breathtaking ride but a triumph of railway engineering which links the eastern and the western coasts of Scotland.

Back on the road, hotels and filling stations are to be found at Garve. Car-weary travellers should always consider the advantages of parking their vehicles and doing a round trip on all or even a part of this rail route.

On branching right at Garve, leaving the A832 and joining the A835, one sees what recent afforestation has done for the bare hills around, and in spring or autumn this part of the route is delightful. To the east, still, is *Ben Wyvis* whose peak is rarely without snow: it is said that, hundreds of years ago, the Ben was allowed to remain independent of the Crown on condition that the King was sent a snowball on every day of the year.

The land to the south east of *Ben Wyvis* is comparatively low lying, and, in clear weather, those who complete the fairly difficult climb are rewarded by outstanding views from the summit.

Beyond *Strath Garve* the A835 turns westwards towards the great *Braemore Forest*. There is some modern re-afforestation here, although it is many thousands of years since this was a forest proper.

Loch Glascarnoch is one of several lochs around Scotland that has been created artificially for hydro-electric purposes. The country around the loch is often cold, windswept and forbidding, and there can be few more uninviting tracks into any of Scotland's dark, scree-covered mountains than those that branch off the road on the stretch between Glascarnoch and the junction with the A832 for Gairloch, shortly before Braemore. Near this junction is the forbidding and gloomy *Corrieshalloch Gorge*, with the spectacular 300-foot *Falls of Measach* easily visited from roadside laybys.

Corrieshalloch Gorge

A diversion — south to Loch Carron

The stretch of the A832 that runs along the southern edge of *Little Loch Broom* and south of *Gruinard Bay* towards Poolewe has been called 'Destitution Road', a nickname which dates back to the time it was built as part of a relief scheme to provide work and food (though not pay) for some of the people hit by the potato famine during the 1850s — an event, incidentally, which is more often related to Ireland than to Scotland, though the effect it had here was almost as great.

The road follows the coastline as closely as any road in the north west and, though it is at times narrow and awkward, this is compensated for by the superb views. At Dundonnell, at the head of *Little Loch Broom* (where there is a 23-room, two star hotel) there are impressive views to the south of some of the weirdly shaped peaks of *An Teallach*.

Following the A832 westwards for eighteen miles, one reaches Aultbea, on the shores of the almost landlocked *Loch Ewe*; a few miles on are the sub-tropical *Inverewe Gardens*. May and June are the best months in which to visit this astonishing place, which was created by Osgood Mackenzie, who bought the estate in 1862. The estate was offered to the National Trust for Scotland by Mackenzie's daughter. The gardens would be beautiful in any setting, but in this wild Highland countryside they appear the more so for being quite unexpected. Not only did the soil have to be especially transported to the site, but trees had to be planted and grown to maturity to give the necessary protection against the elements before flowers and shrubs could thrive. This part of the Scottish coast benefits from the warm current of the *Gulf Stream* giving a generally mild climate here. Over one hundred thousand visitors come every year to see this, one of the outstanding tourist attractions in the north west of Scotland.

From near the village of Poolewe, there are views of *Loch Maree*. Just north of Gairloch, six miles further on, the B8021 branches to the right, towards some of the best bathing beaches on the west coast. At the end of this road lies Melvaig, from where there are views of the Outer Hebridean islands of Harris and Lewis, 25 miles to the west, and of the Shiant Isles, famous for their seabird populations. (There are boat trips

Inverewe Gardens are, like several on Scotland's west coast, 'man-made'. Even the soil was imported in this case. But a mild, westerly, frost-free climate has enabled such places to flourish.

from Scalpay, on Harris — depending on weather conditions — to the Shiants.)

Gairloch has several good hotels, a small harbour and, in its superb setting on *Loch Gairloch* looks out towards Skye and the Outer Hebrides. As well as being a popular tourist resort, Gairloch is a centre for fishing, deer stalking and walking.

Loch Maree, along which the A832 runs for several kilometres, is one of Scotland's most impressive lochs, with several points of interest. On one of the islands in the loch, at more or less its middle point, lived a hermit, *St Maree*, or *Maelrubha*, who gave his name to the loch.

On the north side of the loch is the extremely steep peak of *Slioch* (3215 feet). At the widest part of the loch there is a well-known fishing hotel. Close to the picnic site near the hotel is the start of a *nature trail*, one of two that penetrate the *Ben Eighe Nature Reserve*. The other trail is a 'mountain nature trail' covering about 2½ miles, and is longer than the former.

The A832 continues eastwards from Kinlochewe towards Garve and thus in the direction of the Beauly Firth. Kinlochewe is at the junction of the A832 and the A896, which leads along *Glen Torridon* and *Loch Torridon* to Shieldaig,

with connection roads to remote and beautiful Applecross, which overlooks Raasay, off Skye. There was once a monastery at Applecross, eventually destroyed by the Vikings, which was built by the same Maelrubha who lived on Loch Maree.

The *Torridon Estate* is the property of the National Trust for Scotland, who, as in so many cases, have enhanced the natural appeal of the place by instituting a *Visitor Centre* at the head of *Upper Loch Torridon* and, at the nearby *Warden's House*, a deer museum with live deer in special enclosures.

Until the last few years Applecross and Shieldaig were not easily accessible, but a new road between Kenmore and Applecross reduces their isolation without undermining their beauty. The older road to Applecross, narrow and steep with dramatic 'U' bends, runs from Kishorn to the south east of Applecross. The road negotiates the pass of *Bealach na Ba*, one of the highest mountain passes in Scotland (over 2400 feet).

From Applecross there are fine panoramic views towards Skye and the Cuillins and, five miles south of the village at Toscaig, there is an unexpected link with Kyle of Lochalsh — and thus across to Kyleakin, on Skye itself — in the form of a ferry (passengers only).

The A896 doubles back eastwards from Kishorn to Lochcarron on the shores of *Loch Carron*. Just beyond the village this road joins the A890, which continues along *Glen*

Torridon in winter. This vast tract of land, much of which is in the care of the National Trust for Scotland, is the haunt of wild cats and eagles.

Carron towards Achnasheen, there meeting the A832 on its way towards Garve.

South of Kishorn, at the narrowest point of Loch Carron, are the remains of *Strome Castle*; the castle, a stronghold of the MacDonalds, was destroyed in 1609 by Kenneth Mackenzie, Lord of Kintail. The story goes that the women of the castle emptied water from the well into the gunpowder vat instead of the water vat, thus crippling the castle's defences, and allowing the beseigers to blow it up.

North of Braemore the A835 continues towards the eastern shores of *Loch Broom*, then to Ullapool. Ullapool has been an important fishing settlement for hundreds of years, and although tourism is now very important to the place, the many local and foreign fishing trawlers that dock here and unload their cargoes are far from being merely decorative. Ullapool's significance for the visitor is enhanced by its isolated situation in a dramatically beautiful part of north-west Scotland. It is an embarkation point for cars and passengers travelling to Stornoway on the Isle of Lewis, by ferry (crossing: approximately three hours). There are also summer boat excursions to the *Summer Isles*, and to *Loch Broom*. Ullapool has several good hotels and shops for essential supplies as well as for good quality crafts and the usual souvenirs.

The beautiful *Summer Isles*, lying at the mouth of *Loch Broom*, are virtually uninhabited. They were once as important to the fishing industry as Ullapool, but the herring that were cured once on *Tanera More* and on one or two other islands have long gone. On *Horse Island* there is, inappropriately, a herd of wild goats.

Achiltibuie is another point from which the Summer Isles can be reached. This is a remote, straggling crofting community, idyllic for the summer visitor, but exposed and lonely during the winter months. Achiltibuie is accessible via an unclassified road, well marked, off the A835 approximately ten miles north of Ullapool. A northern arm of this essential network of unclassified roads branches north just beyond *Loch Lurgainn*: it runs towards Lochinver. This road hugs the coast, with exquisite views of sea lochs and lochans and of several peaks, including *Suilven* (2399 feet) which, after Ben Nevis, is probably Scotland's most famous peak.

Here one is on the western edge of the *Inverpolly Nature Reserve*, an idyllic and untamed landscape outstanding even in a part of the country renowned for its natural beauty. The

Ullapool combines the charm of a remote fishing village with the status of a busy but unspoilt tourist resort. There are a few excellent hotels here.

rugged peaks of *Stac Polly* (2009 feet) present a challenge for even skilled climbers. Keeping to the main road, the A835, and continuing northwards along the A837 towards Inchnadamph, one is still on the eastern edge of the reserve. The A837 turns westwards along the northern shore of *Loch Assynt* towards the delightful coastal village of Lochinver. Looking backwards to the east are good views of the much photographed *Ben More Assynt* (3273 feet). All the mountains in this area, including *Quinaig* (2653 feet), *Suilven* (2399 feet), *Canisp* (2779 feet) and *Ben More Assynt* itself, are spectacular, not because of great height, but because they rise steeply from very low land.

There are no real towns in the far north west, so the sizeable villages of Scourie, Kylesku and Durness assume an importance out of proportion to their population.

At *Skiag Bridge*, the road north to Scourie and Durness runs via Unapool and the *Kylesku Ferry*, a five minute, free crossing to Kylestrome. There may be long delays during holiday times, but on this route the crossing is unavoidable.

Those comparatively few visitors who, undaunted by the cost of petrol, venture this far north, reap the reward of the rugged beauty of the wildest and most untamed country in Britain. Some of the mountains here are among the oldest on the earth's surface.

The main road, the A894, is simply the most direct route for local traffic between Kylesku, Scourie and Durness; it has been much improved of recent years. The holidaymaker with time to spare will discover several little-used unclassified roads to such places as Badcall, little more than a handful of crofts above *Badcall Bay*; and north of Scourie, Tarbert, from where, in the summer, there are boat excursions to the cliff-wracked bird sanctuary of *Handa Island*. From the highest points of Handa there are very good views of the mainland mountains.

Scourie is a crofting village with shops for essential supplies, and a hotel. Approximately seven miles east of Scourie is *Laxford Bridge* and the junction with the main road to Lairg, the A832. This road passes no fewer than five lochs along its route. Travelling northwards along the A838 to Durness, a minor road, the B801, runs west from Rhiconich to Kinlochbervie, a charming fishing village. Drive on as far as the road will take you, and if you have the energy, the walk to the beautiful beach at *Sandwood Bay* is well worthwhile.

At Durness there is also a fine sandy beach which is more accessible and will be much enjoyed by summer visitors who can reflect on how crowded such a beach would be south of

Oban or Inverness. Durness has a good, if unpretentious, hotel called the *Far North Hotel*. Formerly an RAF radar station, this is an inexpensive home-from-home. But potential customers should note that for the first ten weeks of the season, which begins in mid May, there are block bookings from parties of bird-watchers. The former radar station also houses a craft 'village', where one can watch craftsmen at work, and buy their goods. Far fewer people who explore the far north coast get to see Cape Wrath than visit John o'Groats, although it is a more impressive, unspoilt landmark. There is a ferry (passengers only) across the *Kyle of Durness* to Keoldale, and, in summer, an hourly minibus service to the Cape itself. The road, all or part of which can be walked by ferry passengers, crosses the northernmost edge of *Parph Moor*, once famous for the packs of wolves that roamed here.

The A838 continues east of Durness, round the head of *Loch Eriboll*, towards the *Kyle of Tongue* to Tongue itself.

At the spacious Victorian *Tongue Hotel* a pair of scales stands in the entrance hall for visiting fishermen to weigh their day's catch. The 18th-century *Tongue House* was originally the home of the chief of the Mackays, but this is now part of the vast estate belonging to the Duke of Sutherland. An even more memorable building is the ruined *Castle Varrich*, believed to have been built by the Vikings. Tongue is not just a spot for fishermen, but one of the best places to stay to see something of this remarkable rocky and sandy north coast.

The A836 that runs almost due south of Tongue towards Lairg, eventually joins the A9. Seventeen miles south of Tongue, on the A836, lies Altnaharra, also well known among fishermen for the quality of salmon and trout fishing in the area. Here the B873 branches to the north west, beginning a lonely path along *Strath Naver*, along the northern shore of *Loch Naver*, before doubling back northwards again to join the A836 near the coast.

Lairg, Dornoch

and the north east

Drivers set on reaching the north coast may well miss the quiet backwater that lies between Lairg and Dornoch, north of the *Dornoch Firth*. It is roughly circumscribed by the railway, so even travellers by train (many of whom will be inspired by the idea of following the famous route to the northernmost railhead in Britain), will miss this self-contained, low-lying corner of the old county of Sutherland.

Dornoch, 22 miles east of Lairg by the A839 and then the A9, may appear to southerners little more than a village; yet it is the principal town of the former county. It is yet another Scottish town distinguished for its golf courses, and the 'Old Course' of the *Royal Dornoch Golf Club* is the most northerly first class course in the world. Visiting players may have a game here, as long as they bring an appropriate letter of introduction; or, less formally, they may play at the other course in the town. There are good sandy beaches at Dornoch and interesting walks around the northern shore of the Dornoch Firth. *Dornoch Cathedral*, built in the 13th century,

but heavily restored in the 19th and later, is said to be the burial place of no fewer than sixteen Dukes of Sutherland.

The alternative route to Dornoch from Lairg is via the A836, southwards, and then the A9. The latter road takes one past the *Falls of Shin* (which has a salmon ladder and a viewing platform) four miles south of Lairg; and a little way beyond there, on the other side of the road, is the ruined *Invershin Castle*, and then *Carbisdale Castle*.

The unclassified road from Dornoch to Embo is a pleasant detour northwards, if time permits, before one joins the A9 for Golspie.

North of Golspie is *Dunrobin Castle*, an unlikely vision of 19th-century elegance, though much restored. Dunrobin is the hereditary seat of the Dukes of Sutherland. Inside the castle are trophies and regimental colours of the *93rd Sutherland Highlanders*, who formed the famous 'thin red line' at the Battle of Balaclava in 1854. The castle is open to the public during the summer.

Dunrobin Castle

Brora, five miles north of Dunrobin, is a whisky-producing town. The most famous product of Brora's distillery is *Clynelish*. The distillery was built in 1819 to provide a market for grain produced by farmers who, evicted from the interior of this part of Scotland, tried to make a home for themselves on the coast. The suggestion of peat in the flavour of Clynelish has led to comparisons with some of the malt whiskies from Islay. Brora has the oldest coal mine in Scotland, whose product, incidentally, first provided power for the distillery.

An unclassified road westwards from Brora strikes towards the hills in the direction of *Loch Brora* and *Strath Brora*. The countryside on the east coast here is much softer and less rugged than on the west, and is most pleasing. This route joins the A839 due west of Golspie. Two miles north of Kintradwell, on the A9, a stone memorial records the killing of the last wolf in Britain.

Helmsdale, a fishing town on the east coast is at the junction of the A9 and the A897 that, once clear of the *Strath of Kildonan* goes due north to Melvich, on the northern coast. There are several places of interest on the A897. Kildonan, nine miles west of Helmsdale, was the scene of a minor goldrush in the mid-19th century, and again in the 1960s, but although gold dust was collected by some people, nothing on a major scale was found.

Kinbrace, like Kildonan, lies on the railway — curious when one remembers that there are villages and even small towns within 40 miles of London that are far less accessible by public transport. The village lies at the junction of the A897 and the B871. The latter, after skirting south of the peaks of *Ben Griam Mhor*, also strikes due north towards the coast.

Back on the A897, the road and the railway part company at Forsinard, and the railway moves north-eastwards across country towards Wick.

The A9 north of Helmsdale continues to run very close to the coast, which is rocky near here. There are castle ruins visible from the road at Berriedale and Dunbeath. South of Latheron, the village of Janetstown, or as it is also known, Latheronwheel, is worth seeing for its secluded old harbour. The Latheron area is rich in prehistoric remains, notably those of *Loch Rangag*, eight miles north of Latheron on the A895. Near Lybster are the *grey cairns of Camster* — well restored neolithic burial chambers which visitors can enter; and further north east along the A9 is the *Hill of Many Stones* near *Mid Clyth*.

A straight line between Wick and Thurso forms the base of a triangle making up the most north-easterly corner of the British mainland. John o'Groats, at the top of the triangle, is popularly supposed to be the most extreme northerly point on the mainland of Britain, and it certainly provides the longest cross-country line from Lands End, in Cornwall. *Dunnet Head*, however, is actually further north by a few miles. Dunnet Head boasts a lighthouse, but does not have hotels and gift shops in which to buy postcards on which one can boast of one's achievements in reaching this famous spot. The name John o'Groats derives, so it is said, from a Dutchman called *John de Groot*, who once ran the ferry to Orkney, several miles north over the Pentland Firth.

In clear weather there are fine views of Orkney, from Dunnet Head as well as John O'Groats, and visitors who are disappointed by the considerable commercialism of the latter might prefer the sheer cliffs and the teeming bird colonies that rise from the foaming sea at Dunnet Head. There are also good sandy beaches at *Dunnet Bay*.

Dunnet Head

Between the two villages lies the *Castle of Mey*, built in 1570, and now belonging to Queen Elizabeth the Queen Mother.

Thousands of southern visitors assume, before they arrive, that this north-eastern extreme of Scotland is mountainous, although a quick look at a relief map will quickly disillusion them even before they travel. Just as chunks of the Highlands seem at times to have been transplanted on to the Lowlands, so inland Caithness seems to belong to some rather more desolate Border country. This part of Scotland is fertile farming country, unassuming and subtle. And depending on one's mood, such scenery can be as invigorating as any lochscape or deserted strath.

Thurso, 500 years ago, was an important trading centre linking Scotland and Scandinavia. Well worth seeing are *Thurso Castle* (exterior view only), *Harold's Tower*, and the *folk museum* that is open during the summer months.

Harold's Tower is a 19th century memorial to the Sinclair family, who, in the 18th century, planned the town of Halkirk, which lies off the A882 between Thurso and Wick.

Wick is a good deal larger than Thurso, quite a holiday resort in its own right, with two good two-star hotels. The existence of the new motel is a good sign of future prosperity for the town. The increase in traffic to Orkney and Shetland that has been occasioned by the oil boom has added to the town's importance. The airport, two miles north east of the town, has regular flights to Orkney and Shetland, as well as Inverness and Aberdeen. The harbour is usually busy with fishing boats, which is another point of interest for visitors who come to enjoy the fine walking along the rocky coast, and for the loch and river fishing, and the golf and swimming. The *Caithness Glass* factory arranges tours for visitors, and the modern factory is another sign of a bright future for the town. Places of interest in the vicinity include the *Noss Head lighthouse* — open at times to the public — (three miles north), and the nearby ruined castles of *Sinclair* and *Girnigoe* (access across the airport runway). Less than two miles south of the town is the ruined *Castle of Old Wick*.

Happily, the future of the rail link to Wick and Thurso seems assured. Though the price of the ordinary return ticket to distant Thurso might seem a large sum this has to be compared to the cost of running a car. It is worth noting too that the various special offers from British Rail can bring the standard price down considerably. One of the most enjoyable long-distance trips in Britain is to take an overnight sleeper to Inverness, then to have breakfast in the Station Hotel there, then take a train from Inverness to Wick or Thurso. The line runs along the *Beauly Firth* to Dingwall, the *Cromarty Firth*, Invergordon, then inland to Lairg, then back towards the North Sea coast before striking inland again, into one of the least populated and most remote parts of western Europe.

SCOTTISH COOKING

Make a taste of Scotland in your own kitchen by using this superb range of cookery books from Johnston & Bacon

Ena Baxter's Scottish Cookbook

by Ena Baxter

This is a new and refreshing approach to Scottish cookery by the expert responsible for many of the dishes made famous by the Scottish food manufacturers, Baxters of Fochabers. Mrs Baxter presents a combination of traditional and modern recipes, setting them against her own Highland background, and insisting on the best Scottish ingredients. 'A fascinating and delightfully-written book in which Ena Baxter gives us the real traditional and country cooking of Scotland from first-hand knowledge'—
KATIE STEWART
96 pages, illustrated with full-colour photographs, 178 x 111mm, paperback, ISBN 0 7179 4560 X, £1.35

Scottish Cooking in Colour

by Dione Pattullo

An exciting new collection of recipes using the many excellent Scottish products — salmon, game, venison, seafoods, soft fruits, oatmeal, and of course, whisky. Traditional recipes have their place here, too — Black Bun, Cranachan, shortbreads, gingerbreads, haggis, bridies. Sumptuously illustrated by colour and line drawings throughout. Foreword by Katie Stewart.
144 pages, 50 colour photographs, 50 line drawings, 246 x 189mm, ISBN 0 7179 4223 6, £4.95

Ena Baxter's Scottish Kitchen Map

This delightful pictorial map is inspired by the recipes of Mrs Ena Baxter, principal of Baxters Foods of Fochabers. In full colour, attractively arranged around a county map of Scotland, are 23 coloured drawings of traditional Scottish dishes and of some of the places after which they are named — for example, Arbroath Smokies and Forfar Bridies. Recipes, too, are included for good Scottish fare.
1010 x 760mm, paper folded in card cover, ISBN 07179 4557 X, 70p

The Best of Scottish Cooking

by Dione Pattullo

A handy and colourful paperback with the more traditional Scottish recipes from *Scottish Cooking in Colour.*
£1.95, 178 x 111mm, paperback

Scotland
~so much to see

. . . and you can see the best of Scotland for only £5.

The Royal Palace at Falkland, with its memories of Mary Queen of Scots. Glenfinnan Monument, where the Jacobite '45 Rising started. Culloden, where it ended bloodily a year later in the last land battle on British soil. Craigievar Castle, which stands today virtually as the masons left it in 1626. Inverewe gardens famed for the South Pacific and Himalayan plants flourishing incredibly on the same latitude as Leningrad. Glen Coe, with its grim memories of the massacre of 1692. The spot on Bannockburn battlefield where King Robert the Bruce is said to have unfurled his battle standard in 1314. Souter Johnnie's Cottage, the home of the Kirkoswald village cobbler, forever immortalised in Burns "Tam o' Shanter".

All priceless parts of Scotland's heritage — cared for and maintained by the National Trust for Scotland. For your £5 annual membership you can visit these — and a further 80 properties, and over 80,000 acres open to the public — without further charge.

The National Trust for Scotland is not, as many people think, a government department. It is a charity, and as such relies solely on its members and supporters to continue its aims of promoting Scotland. Why not become a member?

You can enrol at many of our properties — or fill in the coupon opposite.

I'm interested. Please send me a free colour leaflet ☐

I'd like to become a member ☐ I enclose a cheque/p.o. for £5

Please enrol my family (2 adults & 2 children) for £8 ☐

Name_____

Address_____

_____

_____

THE NATIONAL TRUST FOR SCOTLAND
5 Charlotte Square Edinburgh EH2 4DU 031-226 5922

Orkney and Fair Isle

When visitors to Scotland start to explore some of the outlying islands, they are often heard to say, 'this is like the end of the world'. But they are always wrong. Even if you go to the Outer Hebrides, say, there's still St Kilda eternally lurking 45 miles from the coast of Benbecula, and if you go to Jura, there's still the little sandy, flower-covered and windswept island of Colonsay, the last stop before you reach Newfoundland.

Orkney (or 'the Orkney Islands' — local people don't like the name 'The Orkneys'!) is clearly visible from the northern extreme of Scotland between John o'Groats and Dunnet Head, and here the distance between the two is only about seven miles. So it is not really remote, even though it is coupled in most minds with Shetland — which is 60 miles north of Orkney.

Though they are as far apart as Glasgow and Carlisle and have far fewer similarities than most people expect, Orkney and Shetland share a common past, and perhaps a common future, in the light of North Sea oil development which has radically altered the way of life of these island folk even during the last few years. Such development has proved to be something of a disadvantage to holidaymakers seeking a 'primeval paradise', but has certainly proved of great benefit to the local population.

Orkney has nearly 200 miles of well-surfaced roads, and a permanent population of about 20,000. Kirkwall, on Mainland, has a population of approximately 7000. The pride of this, the capital, is a great cathedral that is owned not by any particular church or sect but by the townspeople themselves. Part of the fabric of St Magnus's cathedral dates back 600 years. The cathedral was founded in 1137, and even then Orkney had been inhabited and had enjoyed a civilisation for hundreds of years.

St Magnus Cathedral

Orkney makes an idyllic hunting ground for the archaeologist and historian. Neolithic relics and ruins are more numerous and better preserved here than anywhere in the British Isles.

There are flights to Orkney and Shetland from Inverness and Aberdeen by British Airways, while on the islands themselves a frequent air-taxi service is operated by Loganair. They run some of the shortest scheduled flights in the world: for example, from Stronsay to Sanday takes only five minutes.

Fair Isle, mid-way between Orkney and Shetland, and administered by Shetland (although included for convenience in this chapter), is inhabited by under 100 people. Though it is a very important staging post for migrating birds, it is still best known for the patterned pullovers produced here. These are made in far fewer numbers than at one time — despite the fact that they once again became fashionable during the 1970s. Some people say that the elaborate and intricate patterns associated with Fair Isle jumpers date back to the Spaniards whose ships were wrecked off Fair Isle during the Armada of 1588.

Fair Isle represents what lonely St Kilda might have been, had the latter's location been less remote.

But Fair Isle is not given over completely to ornithologists. Holidaymakers are welcomed here, though on an island which measures only three miles by two miles they are unlikely to be the kind of people who expect to find city lights and department stores. There is however, colour television.

Orkney

Altogether about one third of Orkney's 70 islands are inhabited. If from a glance at the map the Shetlands look broken and sea-ravaged, then Orkney looks like a piece of crockery that has been smashed to smithereens. Mainland, the principal island, on which the main town of Kirkwall lies, is only about half the size of the Shetland Mainland, although populations are roughly the same.

There are cars for hire on Orkney, but it is still a worthwhile proposition to take your own car from Scrabster, near Thurso (the crossing takes about two hours). Kirkwall is the most unlikely cathedral town in Britain. St Magnus Cathedral was founded in 1127, and there is much sympathetic 19th-century reconstruction, with several most interesting tombs; there is also some 20th-century work.

Opposite the cathedral stands the 17th-century *Bishop's Palace* and the impressive, ruined *Earl Patrick's Palace*; from the top of the great tower of the former there are panoramic views of the town. Nearby is *Tankerness House*, a lovingly preserved merchant's house containing items that trace Orkney's history back over more than 4000 years. Kirkwall's main street, known simply as 'The Street', is busy and interesting, with some ancient houses and attractive well-stocked shops. Visitors about to return home will do well, for example, to stop at *Scot's Fish Shop*, famous for its smoked fish, or at the *Watsons Cheese Shop*: several of Orkney's different cheeses find their way to expensive restaurants in Scotland and England.

The second biggest town on Orkney, also on Mainland, is

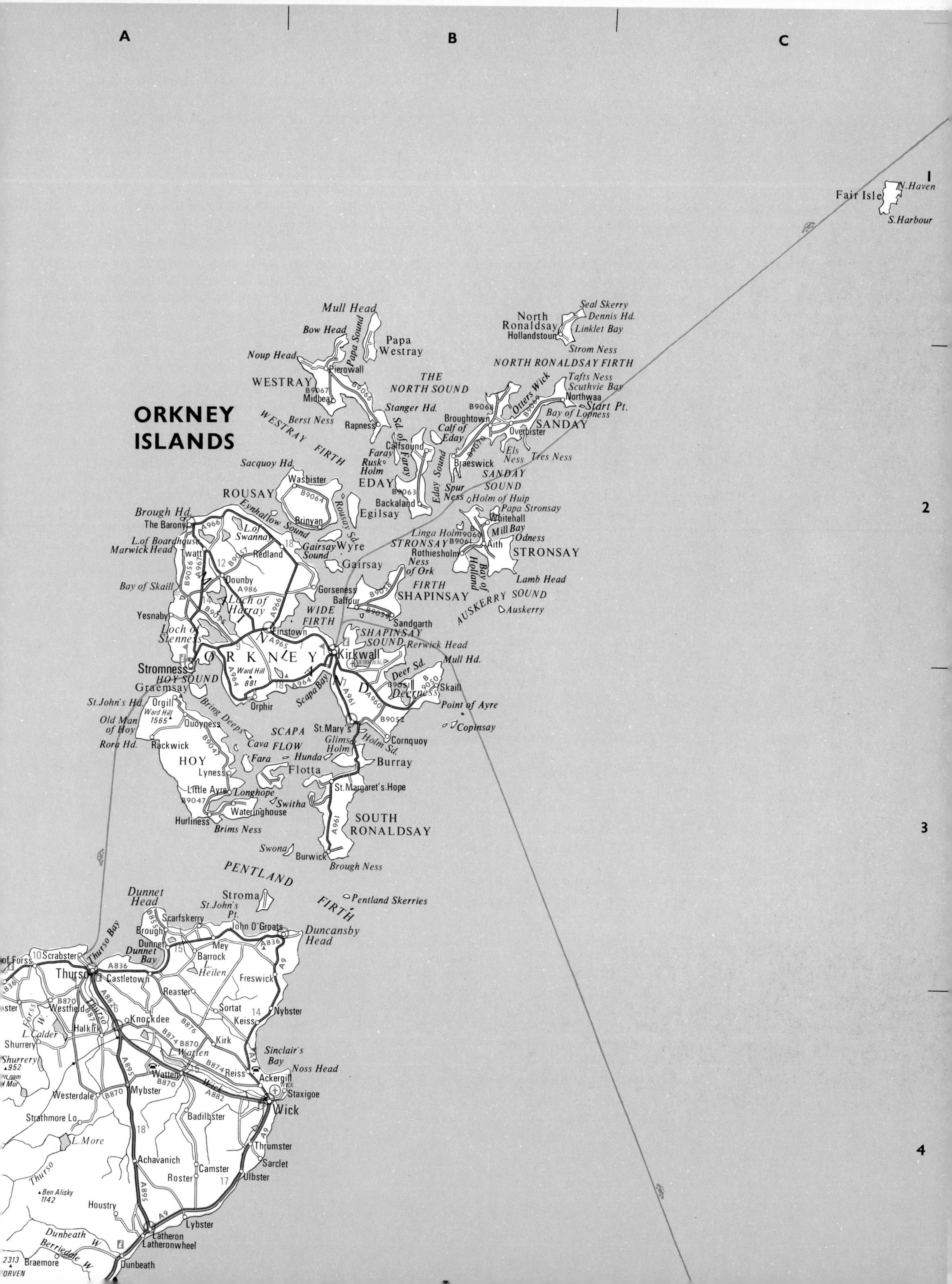

ORKNEY ISLANDS

A   B   C

1

Fair Isle   N.Haven
S.Harbour

Mull Head
Bow Head
Noup Head
Papa
Westray
Pierowall
WESTRAY
Midbea
B9067
B9066
Berst Ness
Stanger Hd.
THE
NORTH SOUND
Rapness

Seal Skerry
Dennis Hd.
North
Ronaldsay
Linklet Bay
Hollandstoun
Strom Ness
NORTH RONALDSAY FIRTH

Tafts Ness
Scuthvie Bay
Northwaa
Start Pt.
Bay of Lopness
SANDAY
Overbister
Els
Ness
Tres Ness

Sacquoy Hd.
WESTRAY FIRTH
Wasbister
ROUSAY
B9064
Brough Hd.
The Barony
A966
L.of Boardhouse
Marwick Head
Twatt
B9056
B9055
12
Redland
Dounby
A986
Bay of Skaill
Yesnaby
B9057
A967
Loch of
Harray
Loch of
Stenness
Stromness
Graemsay
St.John's Hd.
Orgill
Old Man
of Hoy
Ward Hill
1565
Quoyness
Rackwick
Rora Hd.
HOY
Lyness
Little Ayre
Longhope
B9047
Wateringhouse
Hurliness
Brims Ness
Swona
Burwick
Brough Ness

Eynhallow Sound
L.of
Swanna
18
Gairsay
Sound
Gairsay
Brinyan
Rousay Sd.
Egilsay
EDAY
Backaland
Faray
Rusk
Holm
Calfsound
Calf of
Eday
Braeswick
Eday Sound
Spur
Ness
SANDAY
SOUND
Holm of Huip
Linga Holm
B9063
Ness
of Ork
STRONSAY
Rothiesholm
Bay of
Holland
FIRTH
SHAPINSAY
Papa Stronsay
Whitehall
Mill Bay
B9060
B9061
Aith
Odness
STRONSAY
Lamb Head
AUSKERRY SOUND
Auskerry

Gorseness
Balfour
Wyre
Sandgarth
B9058
SHAPINSAY
SOUND
WIDE
FIRTH
Finstown
A965
ORKNEY
MAINLAND
Ward Hill
881
A967
A964
18
A964
Scapa Bay
Orphir
SCAPA
FLOW
Cava
Fara
Hunda
Flotta
St.Mary's
Glimse
Holm
Burray
St.Margaret's.Hope
SOUTH
RONALDSAY

Rerwick Head
Kirkwall
KIRKWALL
Deer Sd.
Mull Hd.
A960
Deerness
B9050
Skaill
Point of Ayre
Copinsay
Holm Sd.
B9052
Cornquoy

2

3

PENTLAND
Dunnet
Head
Stroma
St.John's
Pt.
Pentland Skerries
FIRTH
Scarfskerry
John O'Groats
Duncansby
Head
of Forss
Scrabster
10
Thurso Bay
Brough
Dunnet
Dunnet
Bay
Mey
A836
Barrock
L.
Heilen
Freswick
Thurso
Castletown
A836
15
Reaster
Westfield
Halkirk
Knockdee
B876
Sortat
Keiss
14
Nybster
L.Calder
Shurrery
B874
B870
Kirk
Sinclair's
Bay
Shurrery
952
Westerdale
B870
Mybster
Watten
L.Watten
B874
Reiss
Noss Head
Ackergill
Staxigoe
Wick
Thrumster
Badilbster
Camster
Sarclet
Roster
Ulbster
17
Ben Alisky
1142
Houstry
A9
Dunbeath
Lybster
Latheron
Latheronwheel
Berriedale W
Braemore
2313
ORVEN
Dunbeath

4

Stromness. It was a busy town hundreds of years ago when it was an important port in the trading route between Scotland and the Baltic towns. The aroma from a sweet factory combines with the tang of the fish dock. The *Stromness Hotel*, in the main street, is warm and welcoming and makes a great effort to promote local dishes in its restaurant. Captain Cook is known to have visited the place, and it is believed to have supplied vessels employed in the whaling trade in the 19th century.

About twenty minutes' drive north of Stromness is the important archaeological site of *Skara Brae*. Just as Pompeii was blanketed by molten lava, which preserved much of it intact, so Skara Brae was covered by sand until it was laid bare again by a violent storm in the mid 19th century. Reckoned to be 4000 years old, the village contained beds, hearths, small tools and ornaments, and was one of the most remarkable discoveries made in Scotland. Near Skara Brae are the Bronze Age *Standing Stones of Stenness* and the Ring of Brogar known as the 'Circle of the Sun'. North of Skara Brae, on the west coast of Mainland, is Marwick Head (the B9056 runs close), off which Lord Kitchener was drowned in 1916 when his ship hit a German mine.

Opposite the island of Rousay, on the northern shore of Mainland, is *Gurness Broch*, a Stone Age watch-tower that was adapted by the Vikings as a storehouse and dwelling house, and which is the best preserved on Orkney, and in Scotland. Rousay itself, which is about five miles by three miles, contains more than its fair share of pre-historic sites, especially the *Midhowe Chambered Cairn*, a Neolithic burial cairn more than 75 feet long. The remains of more than 25 people have been found here, in 24 separate burial chambers. There are other cairns on the island, adding to the mystery of an outlying place that communicates an eerie beauty to the layman as well as the archaeologist. Even the tiny uninhabited island of Eynhallow, between Rousay and Mainland, has a ruined church that may have belonged to a Benedictine monastery almost 1000 years ago. And the little Island of Wyre is the home of *Cubbie Roo's Castle*, probably the oldest stone castle in Scotland.

Among the other islands to the north of Mainland are Shapinsay, where the Viking king, Haakon, prepared his ships for the onslaught on the Scottish mainland at Largs: he suffered a crushing defeat when he arrived. Egilsay, a mile east of Rousay, has the well-preserved 12th-century *St Magnus Church*. Its tall round tower is a landmark for miles around. On Stronsay are farms and a fish-processing factory, a reminder to romantics that Orkney is far from being a desolate and uninhabited outpost. The ferry from Kirkwall to Sanday passes close to Eday, and here there are more burial cairns. Sanday itself has one of the largest cairns in the archipelago, over 60 feet long. Westray, one of the largest islands apart from Mainland and Hoy, has a corresponding number of places of interest including two ancient churches, a cave in which some Jacobites hid after being hounded after their terrible defeat at the Battle of Culloden, and the ruins of *Noltland Castle*. Papa Westray, mainly moorland and rough grass is a haunt of wildlife. Here are the remains of the *Knap of Howar*, two substantial stone houses that are believed to be the oldest in Europe. There is a ruined chapel, *The Chapel of St Tredwall*, and a 12th-century church built over what is thought to have been a Celtic monastery 1300 years ago.

The most northerly island on Orkney is North Ronaldsay, with a famous local breed of sheep that, conveniently, thrive on the reddish seaweed that is washed up on the island. There are pre-historic remains, seals, and the tallest lighthouse built on land in Britain — erected 1854 — as well as the remains of a light beacon constructed in 1790.

Scapa Flow, an almost landlocked natural harbour, will always be associated with the scuttling of the ships of the German Navy after their surrender to the British in 1918. Seventy ships, including ten battleships, lay here after being ordered to Scapa Flow, and after some months were sunk or beached by their crews. The harbour, though apparently impregnable, saw the destruction by torpedo of the *HMS Vanguard* in 1917, and of the *HMS Royal Oak* in 1939, both with heavy loss of life. A more peaceful role, though still a maritime one, is now enjoyed by Scapa Flow, for it is of great importance to the oil industry. It is always a scene of activity. The road from Kirkwall to Burwick, near the southernmost tip of South Ronaldsay is constructed partly on top of the concrete blocks that were laid down on the orders of Winston Churchill after the sinking of the *Royal Oak*. Flotta, between Hoy and South Ronaldsay, is a major oil pipeline terminal, hardly beautiful, but still an impressive landmark.

Hoy, the only island on the whole of Orkney with any appreciable hills, is also the biggest of the *South Islands*. There are some impressive cliffs (St John's Head is Britain's highest vertical seacliff at 1136 feet), and the great natural landmark, *The Old Man of Hoy* — a detached red sandstone pillar, 450 feet high.

The Old Man of Hoy

Fair Isle

There are a number of bird sanctuaries on Orkney: at Burwick on South Ronaldsay, on Hoy, at Marwick Head, on Papa Westray and North Ronaldsay. There are also a number of reserves owned by the Royal Society for the Protection of Birds. A number of rare birds are found on Orkney, and the islands are also thronged with seabirds, including fulmars and skuas, and are a major migratory stopping-off point.

Most of the islands in the Orkney archipelago are regularly accessible by ferry and by air — increasingly so as the oil industry becomes more streamlined — and there are boat trips especially designed for the visitor taking in many islands

that have been unaffected by the boom. There are sufficiently good local bus services for visitors not to need to bring their own cars to the islands. Hire cars are available, and these or taxis are best for seeing the pre-historic sites which attract so many travellers to Orkney. Ferry and air services from the Scottish mainland to Orkney are frequent, and are likely to get even better.

Fair Isle

Fair Isle, as Derek Cooper remarks in one of the most fascinating chapters in his book *Hebridean Connection*, 'is as far away from London as Genoa or Prague and much more difficult to reach'. If it were not for the dream of two men, ornithologists George Waterson and Ian Pitman, Fair Isle would, soon after the Second World War, have become depopulated, like St Kilda. Once families leave such islands it is very difficult indeed to repopulate them in later years. The island's name possibly derives from the Viking *Faerey*, meaning sheep, or *Fara*, meaning distant.

The network of air connections that has brought a new and indefinite lease of life to the distant Scottish islands has also saved Fair Isle. Although the famous mail boat *Good Shepherd III* plies between Grutness on Shetland, a six seater plane, though not running a scheduled service, can be chartered. The bird observatory on Fair Isle is perhaps the most remarkable in Britain: over 200 different species have been ringed since work began in 1948. There is room in the hostel here for 28 bird watchers, but it is primarily a place for the convert.

Fair Isle was sold to the *National Trust for Scotland* in 1954, and intending visitors to the island should contact them first (5 Charlotte Square, Edinburgh).

Lamb Holm, Orkney. This 'Italian Chapel' was built in 1943 by Italian prisoners of war. The main structure was based on Nissen huts, the decorations and furnishings were made from scrap metal.

Shetland

Shetland, which was inhabited more than 2000 years before the Romans made tentative efforts to colonise it, was governed by the Vikings from AD 800 until 600 years ago, and of all the Scottish islands that were once dominated by these Norse imperialists, Shetland carries the strongest evidence of their occupation in place names and physical reminders of their presence. Indeed, Shetland has never really severed its connections with Scandinavia. If the Shetlander does not exactly consider himself a Scandinavian, neither does he think of himself as a Scot. Shetland is slightly nearer to Bergen, in Norway, than to Aberdeen.

Shetland brought off something of a coup when the oil-men began to arrive, for the island councillors held out for a healthy share of the land development profits. Generally a tough and independent, down to earth and friendly people, they have made a living from the sea for hundreds of years, against all the odds, and they were not going to be cowed by any 'city slickers'.

Though it is about 70 miles from the northernmost tip of Unst to Sumburgh airport (which has recently had its runway extended — a sure sign of continuing prosperity) the coastline of Shetland is actually nearer 3000 miles — gouged out as it is into hundreds of 'voes', or sea lochs.

While the Orcadians have lived partly off the land and partly from fishing, Shetlanders are traditionally mainly fishermen. In spite of the oil boom there are still expensive trawlers to be seen at anchor in Lerwick harbour.

Shetland still produces luxurious hand-knitted sweaters, and they make a rare souvenir, but nothing quite compares in tourist appeal with midsummer nights in which darkness never falls (by the same token, there are no more than five hours of daylight in midwinter).

The harbour at Lerwick has a modern and international flavour, not just because there are important oil servicing plants here but because fishing trawlers from Scandinavia, Russia and the Baltic ports use the harbour for landing and selling their catches as well as for picking up supplies. There are several very interesting local knitwear shops, and one of the biggest potential tourist attractions in Scotland. This is the annual festival called *Up Helly Aa*, which is held on the last Tuesday of January, and is one of the most photographed and talked about traditional winter festivals in Britain. To celebrate the beginning of the end of the long winter, and the first signs of sunlight that will become stronger and stronger as the spring gets under way, a torchlit replica of a Viking longship is paraded through the streets of Lerwick before being ceremoniously burned in a reconstruction of a Viking funeral rite that celebrated the death of winter.

Fort Charlotte was built in 1665 as a protection against the Dutch; it was burnt by them in 1673, and rebuilt in 1781. It is open to the public.

There is ample tourist accommodation in Lerwick, with two three-star hotels and two two-star hotels, and several smaller establishments. There are several extremely good restaurants.

The A970 links Lerwick and the busy airport of Sumburgh. Here, almost as a bonus for air travellers who have little time to spare on Shetland but want to see something of its past, is *Jarlshof*. This is the excavated site of three villages — a perfect chronology of nearly 3000 years, with fascinating evidence of

Lerwick harbour

Jarlshof

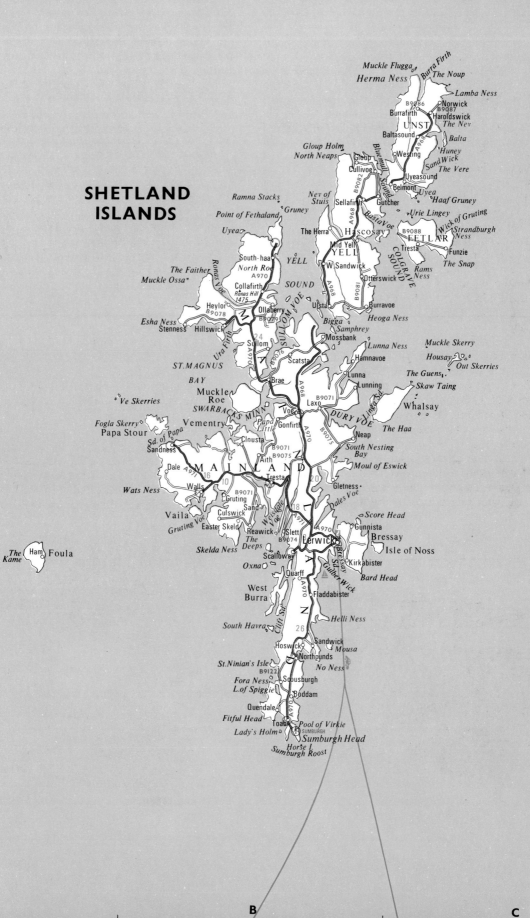

SHETLAND
ISLANDS

Muckle Flugga
Herma Ness
Burra Firth
The Noup
Lamba Ness
B9086 Norwick
Burrafirth B9087 Haroldswick
UNST The Nev
Baltasound Balta
Gloup Holm Westing Huney
North Neaps Gloup Sand Wick
Cullivoe The Vere
Uyeasound
Sellafirth Gutcher Belmont Uyea Haaf Gruney
Ramna Stacks Nev of Stuis
Gruney The Herra Hascosay Urie Lingey Wick of Gruting
Point of Fethaland FETLAR Strandburgh Ness
Uyea Mid Yell Tresta
Funzie
South-haa YELL W Sandwick Rams The Snap
North Roe A970 Ness
The Faither Otterswick COLGRAVE SOUND
Muckle Ossa Collafirth Ulsta
Ronas Hill SOUND Burravoe
Heylor 1475 B9081 Muckle Skerry
B9078 STILLOM Bigga Heoga Ness Housay
Esha Ness Ollaberry Samphrey Out Skerries
Stenness Hillswick Sullom Mossbank Lunna Ness The Guens
B9076 Scatsta Hamnavoe Skaw Taing
ST. MAGNUS Brae Lunna Whalsay
BAY Lunning
Muckle Laxo B9071
Ve Skerries Roe Voe DURY VOE
SWARBACKS MINN Papa The Haa
Fogla Skerry Vementry Little Gonfirth Neap
Papa Stour Clousta South Nesting
Sd. of Papa B9071 A970 Bay
Sandness B9075 Moul of Eswick
Dale A971 Aith Trestal
Walls 10 Gletness
Wats Ness Gruting Dales Voe
B9071 Sand Score Head
Vaila Culswick Gunnista
Gruting Voe Easter Skeld Reawick Bressay
The Slett Lerwick Isle of Noss
Skelda Ness Deeps B9074 Kirkabister
The Scalloway Gulberwick Bard Head
Kame Ham Foula Oxna Quarff
West Fladdabister
Burra A970
N Helli Ness
South Havra
Hoswick Sandwick
St.Ninian's Isle Northpunds Mousa
B9122 No Ness
Fora Ness Scousburgh
L.of Spiggie Boddam
Quendale
Fitful Head Toab Pool of Virkie
Lady's Holm SUMBURGH
Horse I. Sumburgh Head
Sumburgh Roost

domestic occupation through the Bronze Age, the Iron Age and Viking periods. The name is Norse, and there was a Viking settlement here for 500 years, but, sad to relate, the name was actually a fanciful invention by Sir Walter Scott.

In clear weather conditions it is possible to see Fair Isle from the high-lying road just to the north of Sumburgh. The departure point for Fair Isle is from the pier at Grutness, not far from Jarlshof.

Roughly half-way between Lerwick and Sumburgh is the tiny island of Mousa (less than two miles long). Ferries run from Sandwick to Mousa in summer, so that visitors may see the best-preserved Iron Age broch in Scotland.

On the far side of South Mainland, as this part of Shetland is known, lies St Ninian's Isle. Actually just a peninsula joined to the mainland by a spit of white sand, the 'island' was the scene in 1958 of probably the greatest archaeological discovery ever made in Britain. This is known as *St Ninian's Treasure*. Now in the hands of the *National Museum of Antiquities* in Edinburgh, it consists mainly of a haul of silverware, brooches and other valuable Celtic ware that is thought to have been hidden by monks who inhabited a former abbey here when a Viking attack was feared.

Scalloway, the base in the 1940s for rescue operations from under the noses of the German occupation forces in Norway was, until about 200 years ago, the principal town of Shetland. It is now somewhat disfigured by the detritus of the oil boom.

Scalloway Castle was built in 1600 by Patrick Stewart, Earl of Orkney. It is open to the public. The main road passes *Tingwall Valley*, once the setting for the Shetland parliament, the Viking *Althing*, the oldest democratic assembly in the Western world, giving the lie to Westminster's claim to be 'the mother of parliaments'.

The car ferry for the island of Whalsay leaves from Bellisker, about eighteen miles north of Lerwick via the A970 and then the B9075. Perhaps Whalsay is the kind of small island that only visitors with time on their hands get round to seeing, but it is a lively place with a healthy fishing industry and home-produced knitwear. From Whalsay there are passenger ferries to the intriguingly named Out Skerries — the most easterly inhabited outcrop of rocks in the North Isles, with a closely knit population of barely 100 people, who scratch a living from a very barren place.

At Voe the A970, Mainland's principal artery, strikes northwestwards, while the A968 goes almost due north towards the ferry point for Yell, Unst and Fetlar. (Though the road crosses what was until recently bare and lonely

View of mainland Shetland, from Bressay. There is a frequent short ferry crossing from here to near Lerwick, the Shetland capital.

Muckle Flugga and the lighthouse. This is both the northernmost point of Shetland and the northernmost point of the British Isles.

moorland, the country now shows the effects of the oil boom.)

Though Sullom Voe, an unusually deep and secure anchorage, able to accommodate the biggest oil tankers in the world has, perhaps temporarily, had to give natural beauty second place to technology, it is interesting to follow the A970 past Sullom Voe to the north. North of *Ronas Voe* is the landmark of *Ronas Hill* (1475 feet), the highest point in the whole of Shetland. In clear weather it is worth the scramble to the top for the view.

The B9078 runs westwards to Stenness. At Esha Ness are spectacular cliff features called *The Drongs, The Grind of Navir* and the *Holes of Scraada*.

Yell is the biggest of the North Isles. The country is peaty and there are few farms: fishing remains the chief industry.

Apart from Muckle Flugga, whose lighthouse can be visited at certain times, Unst is the northernmost point of Britain. It is comparatively fertile, with prosperous crops, good beaches, hotels and, at Herma Ness, at the north of the island, a nature reserve. There is a landing strip for planes, and enough small industries to keep young people from deserting the island.

According to local legend, the Vikings were so taken with Fetlar that they made this the first colony on the islands. The snowy owl seems to have reacted the same way: in 1967 the first ever pair to breed in Britain set up home on Fetlar and reared several young.

The A971 branches westwards north of Lerwick towards the village of Walls, the embarkation point for the ferry to the remote island of Foula. It continues to Sandness, where thrice weekly boats run to Papa Stour. Papa Stour is best known for its coastal caves, which can be seen by hired boat — though only in calm conditions. Until only 200 years ago there was a leper colony on the tiny neighbouring island of Brei Holm.

Foula, almost as far from the west coast of Shetland as Fair Isle is from the southernmost tip, rises sheer from the sea and, tiny though it is, has five high peaks within its confined area. Only a few families live here, in the company of hundreds of thousands of sea birds, including great skuas, gannets, Manx shearwaters and puffins. There are sheer cliffs on Foula that are a quarter of a mile high.

Even if your sightseeing ambitions in Scotland do not extend as far as Shetland, it is far easier to escape the madding crowd on some small westerly isle or the exhilarating peak of a mountain that poses no danger than most maps may suggest. Shetland is, perhaps, for the more adventurous; further south, even in the Lowlands, travellers who do not like to abandon the security of their cars can experience the splendid isolation that is a vital part of Scotland's magic formula.

91

J&B MAPS

An excellent range of maps from Johnston & Bacon — clear, handy and value for money.

TOURING ROAD MAP OF SCOTLAND
10 miles to 1 inch, 4 colours, plus 8 town
centre plans, £0.75

TOURING ROAD MAP OF GREAT BRITAIN
10 miles to 1 inch, 4 colours, Scotland on reverse side, £0.95

ROAD ATLAS OF GREAT BRITAIN
3 miles to 1 inch, 39th printing, now in paperback,
400pp, $8\frac{1}{4}''$ x $5\frac{1}{2}''$, £2.95

For visitors to London:

VISITOR'S MAP OF LONDON
4 colours, 4 miles to 1 inch, street index to 2800 names, £0.65

VISITOR'S POCKET ATLAS OF LONDON
64pp, $5\frac{3}{4}''$ x 4'', 4 col. maps, 4 miles to 1 inch, street index, £0.95

If you are travelling to Ireland:

TOURING ROAD MAP OF IRELAND
10 miles to 1 inch, plus 5 town plans, £1.00

List of Advertisers

General Information

Public Transport inside Scotland

Much of this guide has been written with motorists in mind, but Scotland is better served by public transport even than parts of southern England, for example. Local buses are not just a luxury but actually a life-line for people living in remote parts of the country, and a scheme developed by the post office in the Highlands and Islands means that passengers can travel by *postbus* along with the mail. Postbus schedules dovetail nicely with ferries on most Hebridean islands, and hotels and guest houses are usually geared to them as well. The postbus system is used extensively in many other areas of Scotland also.

Since the main roads in Scotland are well used, and often quite narrow, motorists will not average high speeds, and this makes long distance *buses and coaches*, more of a practical proposition. Their schedules compare well with average driving times. Here are some examples, with the prices that were correct at time of going to press:

Aberdeen to Dundee: 2 to 3 hours, £1.85
Wick to Dingwall: about 5 hours, £4.00
Oban to Inverness: about 4½ hours, £4.40
(all prices for single fares)

Travelling by *train* in Scotland, though more expensive than the bus, can be more exciting than anywhere else in Britain, and the routes from Fort William to Mallaig and Inverness to Kyle of Lochalsh will compare well with any in Europe for scenic beauty. And as such a large proportion of travellers are going for pleasure rather than business, on the longer routes a holiday atmosphere often prevails. Some times and prices:

Inverness to Kyle of Lochalsh: about 3 hours, about £4
Fort William to Mallaig: about 2 hours, about £1.50
Edinburgh to Perth: about 2 hours, about £1.50
(all prices for single fares)

Travel by train is not always expensive. There are special offers and run-about passes that are good value to anybody who is likely to cover a lot of miles by train. These include the *Freedom of Scotland* pass, for 7 or 14 days, the *Runabout Season Ticket*, very suitable for people based in a particular town, and big concessions on day return tickets. Also obtainable are car ferry multiple tickets, and the Highlands and Islands Development Board's *Travelpass*, which entitles you to travel for eight or twelve days on most train, bus and ship services in the region. Investigate the possibilities as far in advance of your holiday as you can.

Car Hire

Since it is such a common practice to take a train, a plane, a ferry (as a passenger) to comparatively remote parts of Scotland, there is nothing unusual about needing a car when you arrive. So car hire is generally well organised and not impractically expensive. Godfrey Davis, Hertz and Avis are well represented in the main cities, but smaller companies, often with just a handful of vehicles, look after the islands. Orkney and Shetland are especially well provided for. As well as very efficient taxi services, it is possible also to hire a car with a driver, even on a long-distance trip, as you would a taxi.

Travel by Plane

Air travel within the south of Britain is still regarded as something of a luxury, as there are normally alternative methods of transport available. In Scotland it is different; without planes some communities would be cut off for parts of the year, and even under normal conditions families would be separated for long periods. Virtually all the inhabited islands have air links, sometimes on a privately run or for-private-hire basis (though not often), and there are quick links between the main cities and, for example, Orkney and Shetland. In outlying parts of Scotland people look on planes as others would buses. For connoisseurs of the remarkable, the two minute flight from Westray to Papa Westray, on Orkney, is the shortest in the world.

Coach Travel

Not only is getting to Scotland by coach the cheapest way, but the visitor who does not have a car will find that excursion and long-distance coach travel within the country is well organised and co-ordinated. Except in the really remote parts of the country, one is never far from a resort from which one- or two-day coach tours are run. And if one puts up with the need to fit in with pre-ordained schedules there is the great advantage of letting someone else do the driving over sometimes difficult terrain, and of taking a leisurely look at the scenery without having to navigate.

Holiday Cruises

It is possible, of course, to charter a sea-going yacht and crew for a grand tour of the Scottish Islands, but more people will opt for a tour with one of the many Scottish ferry operators, round the Firth of Clyde or the island of Bute, a trip up Loch Katrine on the SS Walter Scott, an outing on the Waverley, the last ocean-going paddle steamer in the world (Scottish High Tea included), or a trip on Loch Lomond. You can go monster-spotting on Loch Ness, take a two- or three-hour cruise down the Caledonian Canal, with a couple of castles thrown in, have dinner on a Union Canal Boat, or go to the spectacular island of Staffa, off the Isle of Mull. There are many options, all worth investigating.

Boating on the West Coast

Yachting — at all levels of skill and experience — is as good off the west coast of Scotland as anywhere in Britain. By taking a boating holiday, even if it is with a sailing school — and you will be discouraged from sailing or cruising unless you can prove some degree of competence — you will be able to visit lochs and islands that are quite inaccessible without a boat. Among several sailing schools are the *Tighnabruaich*, at Tighnabruaich, Argyll, the *Arden Yacht Centre*, Ardfern, Argyll, and the *Glenachulish Sailing School*, House in the Wood, Glenachulish, Ballachulish, Argyll. Even if you have no wish to hire or charter a boat of your own, there are a great many places on the west coast (and to a lesser extent elsewhere) where there are excursions for holidaymakers into otherwise inaccessible places. These are often only known of locally, and are sometimes arranged by hotels for their customers.

Deer-stalking and Shooting

Sportsmen from all over Europe and North America find some of the world's best grouse, pheasant and partridge shooting in Scotland; and the need to cull the resident deer population means that, treated correctly, deer stalking in the Highlands is a satisfying and not a cruel sport. Both are, of course, expensive. Detailed information can be obtained from the Scottish Tourist Board or from *Sport in Scotland, 22 Market Brae, Inverness*, or *Major Ramsay & Co, Farlayer, Aberfeldy, Perthshire*, among others. There are about 100 hotels in Scotland with shooting or stalking facilities, or both. The most famous among these include the *Forsinard Hotel*, Forsinard, Sutherland, Tel. Halladale 221; *Loch Torridon Hotel*, Strathcarron, Ross and Cromarty, Tel. Torridon 242; the *Lochboisdale Hotel*, Lochboisdale, South Uist, Tel. Lochboisdale 332.

Sea-angling, Coarse-fishing and Game-fishing

The view of a lone angler standing mid-stream against a background of wild hills graces many a Scottish calendar. Except for the very best salmon fishing, angling in Scotland is cheaper than most people expect — and much of it is even free. Almost nowhere in Scotland is one far from a trout stream or from the sea. As in the case of stalking and shooting, many hotels and guest houses specialise in fishing holidays, and several hotels and angling/recreation centres offer courses for beginners — such as the *Tweed Valley Hotel Outdoor Recreation Centre, Walkerburn, Peebles-shire*, Tel. Walkerburn 220, and the *Osprey Fishing School, Insch, by Kingussie, Inverness-shire*, Tel. Kingussie 407. Information about sea-angling can be obtained from the *Scottish Federation of Sea Anglers, 8 Frederick Street, Edinburgh*.

Outward Bound, Sporting and Activity Holidays

There are many organisations that cater for mountaineering, hill-walking, yachting, orienteering, canoeing, pony-trekking and riding, rock-climbing, diving, field-studying and more, including courses and sports that are not as commonly associated with the Scottish countryside as the above. Details are best obtained from the Scottish Tourist Board or any regional or local tourist information centres. In most cases, complete beginners and families with children will find something to match their interest.

Special Events

As well as some long-established annual events such as the Edinburgh Festival (late August and early September), the Pitlochry Festival, the Royal Highland Show (in June), and the Highland Games that take place in the late summer and autumn, every region of Scotland has a great many special events of interest to the visitor. Most of these are well advertised locally (regional or local newspapers and local radio are a good source of information) but good advance information can be had from Scottish Tourist Board information centres. You are never far from one of these in any area that attracts tourists.

Tourist Information

In addition to the councils listed here, there is a network of information centres, which provides among other things, assistance with accommodation.

Borders Regional Council, Dept. of Planning and Development — Tourism, Regional Headquarters, Newtown St Boswells.

Central Regional Council, Tourist Department, Viewforth, Stirling.

Dumfries and Galloway Tourist Association, Douglas House, Newton Stewart.

Fife Tourist Authority, Fife House, North Street, Glenrothes.

Grampian Regional Council, The Leisure, Recreation and Tourism Dept., Woodhill House, Ashgrove Road West, Aberdeen.

Highlands and Islands Development Board, PO Box 7, Bridge House, Bank Street, Inverness.

Lothian Regional Council, Dept. of Recreation and Leisure, 40 Torphichen Street, Edinburgh.

Strathclyde Regional Council, Dept. of Leisure and Recreation, Viceroy House, 20 India Street, Glasgow G2.

Tayside Regional Council, Dept. Recreation and Tourism, Tayside House, 26–28 Crichton Street, Dundee DD1.

The National Trust for Scotland

The National Trust for Scotland (note the preposition) has for almost half a century been the guardian of some of the country's finest castles, gardens, country houses, countryside, islands, military sites and more. Since its beginnings in 1931 it has assumed responsibility for 80 properties. Its income comes not from Government funds, but from gifts, legacies and members' subscriptions. Membership at present costs £5 per adult, and £8 for family subscriptions, and allows access to all National Trust Properties in England, Scotland and Wales. Further details from *The National Trust for Scotland, 5 Charlotte Square, Edinburgh.*

Gardens to Visit

Castles and great houses are more readily associated in visitors' minds with the Scottish countryside than gardens, but certain characteristics of the Scottish climate, plus the fact that there has been space to play with and landowners with time and money to spare, have produced a splendid variety of gardens. Some of the best (such as Brodick, on Arran; Crathes, on Royal Deeside; Inveresk, near Musselburgh; Threave, near Castle Douglas) are in the hands of the National Trust for Scotland, but there are also fine Botanic Gardens in Stranraer, Glasgow, Edinburgh and Dunoon, and scores of privately owned gardens that are open frequently for just a day or two each summer. A booklet, price about 40p is available from *The General Organiser, Scotland's Garden Scheme, 26 Castle Terrace, Edinburgh.*

Souvenir Hunting

Shops in all the major cities and tourist centres in Scotland cater for souvenir gifts of all sorts and all prices. Mass-produced 'tartan' goods are available everywhere, but do consider some of the excellent craftsman-made goods — glassware, pottery, silverware, wood carvings, leatherwork, textiles and hornware. If this kind of souvenir does not appeal, the Scots' pride in their country also manifests itself in a magnificent number of topographical and guide books, map folders, books and booklets for motorists, local histories, clan chronicles, memorabilia by well-known Scottish writers, entertainers and personalities. Even some of the smaller tourist information offices keep a good stock of these. The best guide to specific crafts is Johnston & Bacon's pocket-sized book, *Scottish Crafts and Craftsmen*, by Michael Brander.

The Taste of Scotland

Traditional Scottish dishes are now more widely served in restaurants than they used to be — thanks partly to the Scottish Tourist Board's *Taste of Scotland* scheme. Look out for Cullen Skink, a fish broth made with Finnan Haddock, potatoes, onions and milk, and for salmon, kippers and Arbroath Smokies. Venison is worth trying, and Shetland Lamb is an unusual delicacy if you can find it. Haggis is a must — even in the shape of a 'Haggis supper' from a fish and chip shop. Scotland is famed for its baking, of course, and it is impossible to resist the mounds of scones, pancakes and shortbread served up with your afternoon tea.

For cooks who want to try the recipes at home, *Ena Baxter's Scottish Cookbook*, an inexpensive pocket book concentrating on traditional recipes, and *Scottish Cooking in Colour* by Dione Pattullo, a more lavish and adventurous book, are worth investing in. Both published by Johnston & Bacon.

The Water of Life

Whisky (Scotch whisky, that is) is one of the purest and, many would claim, the best, drinks in the world. Versatile and infinitely varied, it is closely linked with the historic past and the economic future of Scotland; and it is a matter of quiet satisfaction to the Scots that imitators all over the world have failed to recreate its magical qualities, lacking as they do the peat moors and the heather, the climate, the raw ingredients and the know-how, imbued in many generations of distillers, that makes whisky what it is.

There are over 3000 brands of blended whisky, compared with about 65 malts. Blended whisky is made from a mixture of malted and unmalted barley, rye and maize, while 'malt' whisky is and always has been made from malted barley alone. The process is much slower than distilling blended whisky, and this tends to make malt whisky so much more expensive. A visit to a distillery is well worthwhile. One practical tip: for various reasons, a 'dram' of malt whisky in a bar costs only a few pennies more than blended whisky, even though the cost by the bottle can be twice as high.

For more information, read *A Guide to Scotch Whisky* by Michael Brander, published by Johnston & Bacon.

Kilts and Tartans

The *Scottish Tartans' Society Museum of Tartans*, in Comrie, Perthshire (on the A85, a few miles west of Crieff) houses the biggest collection of material on tartans and Highland dress in the world. Their earliest tartan is a fragment that dates from AD 245, the so-called Falkirk Tartan, which was found stuffed in a jar of coins in Falkirk. At the Pitlochry factory of A & J Macnaughton, visitors can see tartans being made. The firm was founded in 1791, and is believed to be the oldest company of its kind in the world. There are many books and leaflets about tartans, and even if you never wear a kilt or even a tartan scarf, it is fun to be able to identify at least the commonest tartans.

94

Highland Games

The first Highland Games are said to have been convened at Braemar by Malcolm Canmore, an 11th-century King of Scotland. The *Braemar Highland Gathering* is probably the best known in Scotland, partly because it is regularly attended by the Royal Family. But there are other places in which to witness the tossing of the caber. Among the best are those at Edinburgh, Dunoon, Aboyne, Oban, Perth and Peebles. All of these take place in the autumn. And in addition to these famous gatherings, many small towns organise their own games, in which music and dancing seem to play as big a part as sports.

Live Entertainment

The larger holiday resorts such as Rothesay, Oban, Aberdeen and Dunoon stage lively summer shows, but even in smaller places there are less formal *ceilidhs* and folk evenings, in bars, hotels, even local community halls. This is especially true of the islands, where people are more used to organising their own entertainment. Outsiders are always welcome, and they do not have to participate — they can just sit and nurse a dram . . . . There are well established theatres in Pitlochry, St Andrews, Stirling, on the Isle of Mull, Inverness and elsewhere.

In Famous Footsteps

You will not get far in Scotland without coming across Robert Burns or Mary Queen of Scots, Robert the Bruce or Bonnie Prince Charlie, Dr Johnson and James Boswell or Sir Walter Scott — not in the flesh, but in one manifestation or another: as statues, ghosts of some great castle or mansion, inspiration of some museum or visitor centre, centrepiece of a literary festival or a country bookshop display. Large tracts of the Border country are linked with the characters of Scott's novels, for example, Mary Queen of Scots and Robert the Bruce seem to have visited an impossible number of places. Johnson, who did not visit Scotland until he was nearly 65, and his biographer and confidant, James Boswell, were among the first 'tourists' ever to set foot in the Highlands, and virtually pioneers when it came to exploring the Western Isles. The ambitious visitor can follow all or part of the journey described in Johnson's 'A Journey to the Western Isles' and Boswell's 'Journal of a Tour to the Hebrides'. The stories of Robert Burns and Prince Charles Edward Stuart, or, as he is more generally known 'Bonnie Prince Charlie', are both coloured with sentimentality: but strip away the nonsense, and both men are fascinating — well worth the status of folk heroes. The stories of all these figures are neatly contained in a booklet published by the Scottish Tourist Board called *Scotland in Famous Footsteps*.

The High Road, and the Low Road

The old song is familiar enough: 'Ye tak' the High Road and I'll tak' the Low Road, and I'll be in Scotland afore ye'. But not everybody who hears it realises that the refrain has nothing to do with the new by-pass. The Low Road is the singer's allusion to the road that his soul will take after his death. Either way, alive or dead, he belongs in Scotland . . . .

'Nessie', and Other Monsters

There cannot be many people who pass Loch Ness without a sidelong glance at the water, *just in case* they spot 'the monster'. Belief in the creature lurking in the depths lingers on: Peter Scott, the respected naturalist, lends credence to the idea by adding his voice to those of the converted. Most tourist information bureaux have books and brochures about the Loch Ness Monster — among the best of which are the paperback by investigator Tim Dinsdale, and the decorative and informative sheet map by the same author, published by Johnston & Bacon.

Many other sea and inland lochs have strange creatures associated with them, the most seriously treated of which is 'Morag', who is believed to live in the deep waters of Loch Morar. Happy hunting!

Acknowledgements

The publishers wish to thank the Scottish Tourist Board and the many regional tourist offices who gave advice and assistance.

The illustrations were kindly supplied by the following people: the drawings on pages 6, 7, 8, 19, 20 (except Buckie House), 27, 29, 39, 48 (Staffa), 52, 56, 58, 59, and 62 by William Cuthill. The drawings on pages 15, 16, 20 (Buckie House), 21, 36, 38, 44, 48 (Duart Castle), 64, 69, 73, 78, 82, 83, 86, 87, and 88 by Reiver Design Associates Ltd, Galashiels.

The colour pictures were supplied by the following: the illustrations on pages 11, 17, 29, 59, 63, and 66 by the British Tourist Authority. Pages 16, 27, 30, 35, 61, and 87 by the Scottish Tourist Board. Pages 18, 33, 34, 50, 79, and 80 by the National Trust for Scotland. Pages 13, 45, 47, 65, 71 and 81 by Magnus Carter. Pages 23, 37, 43, 51, 68, 70, 72, and 77 by R. Adam Brown. Pages 90 and 91 by Sally Morris.

Maps based upon the Ordnance Survey Map with the sanction of the Controller of H M Stationery Office. Crown Copyright reserved.

Cover: Urquhart Castle, Loch Ness (by Magnus Carter); Pipers at St Fillans (by Magnus Carter); the Pap of Glen Coe (by R. Adam Brown).

Index

96

97